Jim Crow of the Mind
and
The New State Laws Designed to
Preserve the Idea
of White Male Supremacy

ALSO BY JOHN L. HODGE

BOOKS:

Presidential Racism: The Words of U.S. Presidents Since the Civil War, and an Essay: The Enduring Anti-Democratic Disease Afflicting Us – And its Cure (2020)

Overcoming the Lie of "Race": A Personal, Philosophical, and Political Perspective (Second Edition, 2017)

Dialogues on God: Three Views (2012)

How We Are Our Enemy – And How to Stop: Our Unfinished Task of Fulfilling the Values of Democracy (2011)

Cultural Bases of Racism and Group Oppression: An Examination of Traditional "Western" Concepts, Values and Institutional Structures Which Support Racism, Sexism and Elitism (co-author) (1975)

BOOK CHAPTERS:

"Equality: Beyond Dualism and Oppression," Chapter 6 of *Anatomy of Racism* (1990)

"Democracy and Free Speech: A Normative Theory of Society and Government," Chapter 5 of *The First Amendment Reconsidered* (1982)

JOURNAL ARTICLE:

"Deadlocked-Jury Mistrials, Lesser Included Offenses, and Double Jeopardy: A Proposal to Strengthen the Manifest Necessity Requirement," *Criminal Justice Journal* (Vol. 9, No. 1) (1986)

FOR DETAILS, GO TO: JOHN L. HODGE.COM

Jim Crow of the Mind
and
The New State Laws
Designed to Preserve the Idea
of White Male Supremacy

John L. Hodge
J.D., Ph.D.

Copyright © 2023 by John L. Hodge
All rights reserved.

No part or portion of this book may be reproduced in any manner by any means whatsoever or translated into any language or form by any means whatsoever without the written permission of the author. To obtain written permission, contact the publisher at the email address below.

Published in the U.S.A,
by
John L. Hodge, Publisher
Jamaica Plain, Massachusetts
U.S.A.
Email: JLHPublisher@gmail.com

Cover design and sculpture photographs by John L. Hodge.

Your comments are appreciated. Use the email address above. Order books from local or online retailers.

**For more information,
go to the website at
johnlhodge.com**

ISBN: 978-0-9831790-8-5

Print on demand services provided by Lightning Source, Inc.

**Printed copies available through
local and online book sellers.**

CONTENTS

Preface   1

Chapter 1: Connecting the Dots   11

Chapter 2: Jim Crow and Its Continuing False "Racial" Foundation   27

Chapter 3: Beyond Legality   45

Chapter 4: Components of Jim Crow of the Mind   50

Chapter 5: Texas   67

Chapter 6: Florida   78

Chapter 7: Georgia   87

Chapter 8: Virginia   91

Chapter 9: Tennessee   95

Chapter 10: South Carolina   103

Chapter 11: Alabama   109

Chapter 12: Kentucky   114

Chapter 13: Oklahoma   118

Chapter 14: Iowa   124

Chapter 15: Arkansas   129

Chapter 16: New Hampshire   133

Chapter 17: Montana   138

Chapter 18: South Dakota   144

Chapter 19: North Dakota   149

Chapter 20: The Danger: What Lies Ahead?   152

Acknowledgments   154

Epilogue: Searching for Reality in the Face of Myths and Lies   155

Notes and Sources   162

Index   207

The Author   215

"Who built the seven gates of Thebes?
The books are filled with names of kings.
Was it the kings who hauled the craggy blocks of stone?
. . .
In the evening when the Chinese wall was finished
Where did the masons go? "
                 — Bertolt Brecht, "A Worker Reads History"

Preface

You can be fired if you are a teacher in a public school in any of fifteen states of the United States and discuss the content of the book you have just begun to read. More states may be added to the fifteen after this book's publication.

Imagine yourself as a public school teacher. There are thousands of books like this one that you cannot discuss in the classroom without jeopardizing your job in these states. You should probably not be seen reading any of these books in public. Word could get around to the people who hired you to teach. The states' political leaders encourage people to report anyone suspected of violating these new laws. You never know who may be watching and ready to report.

Together the fifteen states represent 32% of the Electoral College — enough to impact the outcome of any presidential election — 30% of the U.S. Senate, and 32% of the U.S. House of Representatives. So this is not just about the teachers and students in fifteen states but about the future of democracy in America — which will impact the future of democracy throughout the world.

In these states, students will be deprived of the ideas contained in these books. They will have truncated minds constricted to conventional things. They will be open to hearing that any words challenging convention are spoken by evil people who are socialists, heathens, liberals, or just Democrats. This is happening now. Such assertions are proclaimed by many top officials not only in these fifteen states but throughout much of the country.

The books that are banned and the open discussion of their ideas that are thwarted are about the pervasive impact of the legacy of racism and sexism in America. The proponents of these banning laws call them a prohibition against "critical race theory." But most of these laws are also prohibitions against discussion of sexism and women's right to choose as well as against any thoughtful analysis of how slavery, racial segregation, and oppression of women have plagued American society throughout its history and continue to do so.

Here I focus on racism and sexism, but I recognize that the laws of some states that ban discussion of gay and transgender issues are just as repugnant, as are the laws that restrict the ability to vote.

To be fair to you dear reader, I must disclose my personal interest in eliminating the laws that ban books and restrict discussion. It is simply a matter of ethics that writers who have a financial or personal interest in the subjects they are writing about should disclose that interest to the readers. As I will explain, I am personally affected by these laws, for the writings that could be banned according to these laws include books and essays that I have written over the past half-century, including this one. In my view, I am writing to protect freedom of speech and democracy itself, but that may be just a self-deceiving way to cover up my personal bias, so you should know about my personal interest too.

In 1975 with two co-authors I wrote and published my first book: *Cultural Bases of Racism and Group Oppression: An Examination of Traditional "Western" Concepts, Values and Institutional Structures Which Support Racism, Sexism and Elitism*. In the Preface I stated:

> The elite group which traditionally rules in Western societies, and which still continues to rule in

"democracies" such as the United States, is drawn mostly from the ranks of upper-class white males. For this reason this book is also a study of the values and norms which have supported white male supremacy. The result of this elite rule is group oppression. . . . The term "group oppression" . . . includes racism within its meaning.

Such a statement would likely be banned by the state laws examined here. Since the statement is an overview of much of the content of the book, it means that the whole book and any ideas attributed to it can be similarly banned. In addition, the book exposes the entrenched sexism and racism-like superior groupism of "Western" thinkers deemed by authoritative figures to be among the most important contributors to "Western" civilization, from Plato to Freud. These famous men rationalized sexism and racism by postulating a metaphysical hierarchical dualism that pitted superior rationality represented by "white" males (themselves) against inferior emotion.

This is an example of how these state laws could adversely affect me. Here are more examples:

In the Epilogue of *Overcoming the Lie of "Race": A Personal, Philosophical, and Political Perspective* (second edition), I wrote:

> The United States was founded, in part, to preserve slavery. That is its legacy. This legacy is quite visible today and stands in the way of the nation's further advancement towards fulfilling the values of democracy, values that respect and honor the humanity of every human being. . . .
>
> The American Revolution that freed the American colonies from British rule would not have occurred or succeeded without the support of the

southern states whose main goal was to preserve slavery.

These statements, which in my view are well documented and state the truth, would conflict with what is permitted by the state laws examined here. In these states—and in others that may adopt similar laws—a book containing such statements could be banned from the public schools.

In 2020 I wrote and published *Presidential Racism: The Words of U.S. Presidents Since the Civil War*. In the Preface I wrote:

> The racism is not only that of the presidents ... but also that of the dominant forces of the society that put these men in office and promoted, tolerated, or turned a blind eye to the racist policies that ensued. The presidents, in turn, reinforced that society-wide racism through statements and policies that rippled throughout the society. It is notable that the racist views of 2020 differ little from those of 1866.

The state laws examined here could easily be interpreted to ban such critical assessments of United States presidents. The book quotes the presidents, so there is no question about the accuracy of their views. But historical accuracy would often be banned by these laws if they do not reflect a rosy view of United States history. The state governments that have enacted these laws are little different from China where the history taught in schools is the rosy fantasy of the Communist Party, having little to do with empirically established facts.

In addition, two newspapers respected for quality journalism—the *Washington Post* on July 8, 2018, and the *Boston Globe* on June 13, 2021—published online my letters to the editor explaining that the American War of

Independence that severed the colonies from British rule was fought and won, in part, to preserve slavery. These letters might have interfered with many Americans' desires to feel good about their country. The state laws examined here are designed to prohibit discussion of this matter.

These state laws are not limited to suppression of discussion of the United States' racist history. Many also suppress exploration of sexism, and thereby also suppress discussion of the sordid history of the oppression of women including taking away women's control over their own bodies. Most of these same states have strict laws prohibiting abortions.

More than a decade before the overturning of *Roe* v. *Wade*, I outlined the oppressiveness of what would happen if the idea of human life beginning at conception were to take hold—as it now has in most of these states. For example, I stated in Chapter 5 my book, *How We Are Our Enemy – And How to Stop*:

> The "pro-life" view regards the fetus as a living being from conception, which is before the pregnant woman knows that she is pregnant. Logically, the "pro-life" view means that government would be obligated to protect the fertilized egg as soon as it is fertilized in the same way that the government protects children. To accomplish this, the government would have to monitor every woman of child-bearing age and either monitor their sexual activity or subject them to regular examinations to determine whether they are carrying a fertilized egg. Then, once [the] fertilized egg is detected, the pregnant woman's way of living would be subject to government oversight. . . . She would be instructed on how to live to preserve the fetus, and any intentional failure to follow these instructions

would potentially subject her to criminal prosecution and, if the fertilized egg dies, potentially the death penalty . . . a consequence appropriate for a horrifying tale of science fiction — but this potential is not fiction.

Critical discussion of this would be prohibited under the laws of most of these states. In addition, the book expands the inquiry contained in *Cultural Bases of Racism and Group Oppression*.

Since these laws seek to suppress awareness of what I have written, you can see why I might be regarded as biased. But what might be seen as my bias is a point of view about European and American culture and history resulting from my decades of study and empirical observations, a point of view that I first published nearly fifty years ago when I explained why racism and sexism are so deeply ingrained in our society and culture. My view sees racism and sexism as connected like two sides of the same coin. The coin itself, as I discuss in Chapter 1, is the myth of superior "white" male rationality.

But there is a much bigger issue than the writer's potential bias. It is freedom of expression.

While my writings have been critical of "Western" or Anglo-European culture for its ingrained racism and sexism, at the same time I recognize that the writing and publishing of my critical views is acceptable within this culture and would not be acceptable in many parts of the world where similar problems exist. The need for freedom of expression is an essential ingredient of this culture, though it is also constantly threatened. The defeat of Hitler in World War II, for example, was necessary to maintain it.

The need for freedom of expression was clearly and forcefully stated by John Stuart Mill with the publication of

On Liberty in 1859. (Mill credited Harriet Taylor Mill, his wife, for providing many of his ideas.) But the value of freedom of expression was acknowledged much earlier in places like the Netherlands, particularly in and around Amsterdam, where in the seventeenth century Descartes and Spinoza could freely write their new ideas without oppression, and where in the seventeenth and eighteenth centuries Portuguese and Spanish Jews went to survive and freely practice their religion. The Pilgrims who came to America in 1620 to escape persecution in England first went to Leiden in the Netherlands before embarking on their adventure across the ocean. Similarly in England in the early seventeenth century, Francis Bacon, and later that century Isaac Newton, could present world-changing new ideas without the harassment suffered by Galileo in Italy. The Englishman Roger Williams, in the early seventeenth century, introduced the idea of separation of religion from government, an idea that was later incorporated into the First Amendment of the United States Constitution, ratified as part of the Bill of Rights in 1791. The separation of religion from government is an essential component of freedom of expression, for religions historically have been notorious for punishing and killing those who do not agree with the religion.

But many persistent ancient ways of thinking remain in the present that seek to preserve the pre-Renaissance past when religion and the state combined to preserve rigidly hierarchical societies and suppress any opposition. They accomplished this by treating new ideas as heretical and by attacking dissidents. Proponents of new ideas were subjected to persecution and many times, death.

For example, Roger Williams was banished from the Massachusetts and Plymouth Bay colonies in 1636 for opinions deemed unacceptable. He obtained an agreement with the indigenous people to settle in a place he named

Providence in what later became Rhode Island. His unacceptable opinions included separation of church and state, freedom of speech, the banning of slavery, and respect for the indigenous people. Many others moved to join him. But after he died, the old hierarchical ways of thinking re-emerged. The city renounced his new ideas and by the end of the eighteenth century Providence had become a major center of the slave trade.

It is an unfortunate pattern whereby the oppressive past reasserts itself to thwart progressive ways of thinking and behavior. The more progressive ways often prevail many decades or centuries later, but the ways of the past still linger and threaten the future.

Another example: Prior racists beliefs re-emerged throughout the country soon after the Thirteenth Amendment abolished slavery, beliefs that effectively led to apartheid in many states for nearly a hundred years after slavery was abolished. The apartheid has been glossed over by calling it "Jim Crow." The U.S. Supreme Court decision of *Plessy* v. *Ferguson* in 1896 ratified pre-existing legalized apartheid prevalent in southern states. This American apartheid preceded apartheid in South Africa by many decades.

Then, in the twentieth century while segregation and apartheid continued in the United States, racist and sexist beliefs ballooned in Europe in the form of Nazism and Fascism, threatening to return Europe to the Dark Ages. Under Nazism and Fascism, dissenters were imprisoned or killed. Racist genocide followed: the Holocaust.

These ancient ways of thinking are present today. They reject democracy and promote hierarchically ruled societies. These hierarchical ways of thinking are evident in the recent state laws that I examine here. They are the outcome of persistent ancient beliefs that reject democracy and the values that underlie it.

Democratic values are derived from the logic of the golden rule. The rejection of this logic is a rejection of the idea of human equality, the idea upon which democracy is based. I explained the logical connection between democracy and the golden rule in both *Presidential Racism* and *How We Are Our Enemy--And How to Stop: Our Unfinished Task of Fulfilling the Values of Democracy*.

If equality is rejected, racism, sexism, and rule by a corporate elite or an authoritarian dictator is then permitted. To reject equality, it is essential to deny freedom of expression, for such freedom would permit the oppressed and their supporters to have a voice. For oppression to succeed, the oppressed must not be heard. If the oppressed cannot be heard, their oppression will not be alleviated, their equality will be denied, and democracy will be defeated.

Freedom of expression, separation of government from religion, and non-racist, non-sexist democracy are essential components of the health of humanity. Thus, it is not just that I do not like laws that would ban my books and ideas; I do not like laws that oppose these essential components, for these recent illiberal laws do just that. They not only suppress the views I have been writing about, they also reject the ideas that are necessary for the survival and growth of democracy.

The preceding descriptions of some of my writings give you a glimpse of my long-standing point of view and the potential financial and personal impact on me of the state laws I examine here. Having revealed this and explained the more important reason why I am writing this book, I think my ethical obligation of disclosure has been satisfied.

"All through school the Negro is taught the history of Western Caucasian civilization and almost nothing is included which relates to the ethnic background of his own race."

— Grace Hays Johnson,
"Phases of Cultural History of Significance for Negro Students," *Journal of Negro History* (January 1937) as quoted in Michael Dennis, *Luther P. Jackson and a Life for Civil Rights.*

CHAPTER 1

Connecting the Dots

The new state laws that reinforce Jim Crow of the mind are rooted in hundreds of years of history and mythology. This book begins by addressing these roots so that we can see that these laws are not anachronisms but instead are case studies of the centuries-old and world-wide battle between elitism and democracy. This battle is raging within America today as it has throughout its history.

The interactive components of this battle that I address in this and the next chapter are —

1. The myth of superior "white" male rationality;
2. The "racial" mythology sustained by our language;
3. The need to unite politically around democratic values—but with awareness of society's "racial" distinctions;
4. The continuing historical forces that emanated from slavery and its rationalizations.

We can better comprehend the perils of Jim Crow of the mind when we understand its historical roots.

What is Jim Crow of the Mind?

Jim Crow of the mind is the suppression of points of view that expose the ingrained racism and sexism of American society. It includes the suppression of any expression that reveals the contributions by and the oppression of people who are not "white" males. The sources of the expressions targeted for suppression include books, magazines, and the words of teachers in the classroom. Jim Crow of the mind works by controlling education and information and often includes the banning of books, the firing of teachers, and fearmongering by public officials.

Jim Crow of the mind is not just a distant past event or a future threat but a present reality. It is incorporated into many state laws that are in effect today. The laws of the many states examined here determine what is taught in the public schools. These laws mold future voters. These voters will determine whom the Electoral College will select to be the next president of the United States.

Jim Crow of the mind is a persisting component of **Jim Crow** — the term used to describe the racial segregation that pervaded the United States, North and South, for approximately one hundred years after legal slavery was completely ended in 1865 with the enactment of the Thirteenth Amendment to the U.S. Constitution. To be clear, segregation was not just about the *separation* of "whites" from non-"whites"; it was about the *oppression* of non-"whites." This oppression was enabled by federal, state and local laws that the courts found were proper. The primary victims of this oppression were people of African ancestry, Asians, and indigenous peoples.

Jim Crow, as explained in the next chapter, was both physical and mental. Since legalized physical segregation is now outlawed by federal laws and Supreme Court decisions (which could change), there is a subsequent mission to segregate our minds: on one side, ideas that are conventional and uncritical, and on the other, ideas that expose and oppose the tacit acceptance of the idea of white male supremacy.

This oppression of the mind suppresses ideas. Since ideas have no "race," color or gender, this suppression evades direct and obvious violation of the laws barring "race" and gender discrimination. The impact is discriminatory nonetheless and represents a resurgence of the idea of white male supremacy as the tacit and usually unspoken ideology of much of the land.

Although I focus here on laws affecting education, it is important to realize that these laws are part of a larger body of oppressive laws that suppress the ability to vote, stifle awareness of gays, and deny women the equal right to decide for themselves what happens to their own bodies. These oppressive laws are part of a national mission to reverse the growth of human rights and to nullify the idea of universal human rights. Many states already use various mechanisms to restrict the ability to vote, so what is now in progress is a rejection of the fundamental idea, expressed in the Declaration of Independence, that governments derive "their just powers from the consent of the governed." Continued Jim Crow of the mind is an essential component of this broader mission.

The laws that I address here are billed as suppressing an evil that is called "critical race theory." This evil is most often attributed to "Black" writers. But most of these laws suppress feminism as well. These laws are currently concentrated in the South, but they have extended as far north as Iowa, Montana, New Hampshire, North Dakota and South Dakota. This is Jim Crow of the mind, the new effort to segregate and suppress points of view that expose and oppose the idea of white male supremacy.

How are Racism and Sexism Connected?

The myth of the superiority of the "white race" and the myth of male superiority combine to produce the myth of the superiority of "white" males. The myth means that people not "white" are inferior, and people not male are inferior.

The myth of male superiority is conjoined with the idea that rationality is superior to emotionality and that it is males who are more rational. This idea stems from Plato and Aristotle—who have been portrayed as providing the intellectual foundation of Western culture—and persists today. Sigmund Freud, for example, in *Civilization and its Discontents,* affirmed the historical idea of superior male rationality: "The work of civilization has become increasingly the business of men, it confronts them with ever more difficult tasks and compels them to carry out instinctual sublimations of which women are little capable."

Similarly, European males are presumed to be rationally superior to non-Europeans, so that cultures that are not "white" are regarded as more like women. Who remains at the top? The more rational European or "white" male. There is, of course, no rational basis for this idea.

This is how racism and sexism are connected. They are both products of the idea of the superior rationality of the "white" male. (I examined this in depth in *Cultural Bases of Racism and Group Oppression.*)

It is influential and powerful "white" males who decide that it is they who are superior. Their self-serving view of themselves is perpetuated by male political and economic power sustained by laws that they have created to maintain that power. That power is supported and enforced by many powerless "white" males and their powerless wives who like the idea of their superiority and identify with the "white" male elites.

With that power these elites control nearly all aspects of culture, including education and religion, to sustain their view of themselves, creating a mythology that is deeply ingrained in the unconscious of the culture.

The new state laws examined here are examples. They are frantic attempts to thwart the rising tide of women and the rising tide of people who are not "white." In addition there is a significant minority of "white" males who join this rising tide. They are sensible people who reject the idea of their superiority.

Thus, the new state laws sustaining Jim Crow of the mind are not only about racism but about sexism as well. These laws support the continuation and further building of the tacit idea of white male supremacy as the ideological premise—unconscious and sometimes conscious—of the United States.

We will see in the state-by-state chapters how the laws bar full exploration in public schools into the nation's sexism as well as into its racism. Jim Crow of the mind, by keeping us and our children ignorant of the pervasiveness of racism and sexism, helps perpetuate the oppression of all women, "white" and non-"white," as well as the oppression of all people not considered to be "white." In addition, other laws not discussed here suppress discussion of gay relationships and transgender issues.

It is no arbitrary coincidence that most of the same states that establish Jim Crow of the mind have established laws that deny women any meaningful right to terminate their pregnancies. The denial of that right is a form of sexism in that it prevents women from determining what happens to their own bodies. In addition, most of these same states did not timely ratify the Equal Rights Amendment, which would have made equal rights for women a part of the U.S.

Constitution. Some rescinded their earlier ratifications. Their failures to ratify the ERA makes these states official supporters of male supremacy.

How Our Language Perpetuates False "Racial" Distinctions

Today we are all still slaves to the language of slavery. I will explain and make a change.

The idea of "race" is a political tool used by those in power to maintain a hierarchical society that helps those in power to stay in power. The idea began to emerge in the laws of some American colonies over 350 years ago. It was used to justify slavery, often portraying "Blacks" as biologically inferior and little more than non-human animals.

That political tool has survived and is incorporated into our daily language and is still used to keep the population divided into silos. That division stifles efforts to unite those who are oppressed. There are some people called "Black" who are antisemitic. "White" women are often stereotyped as "Karens," thereby separating them from other women, all of whom suffer from sexism. "White" people are lumped together as privileged whether they are gay, disabled, women, impoverished, or victims of abuse. Unconsciously (mostly), "Blacks" are seen as more suited to service roles, sports, or entertainment than to science or positions of leadership. These are just a few of many possible examples.

There are exceptions, of course—and over many decades the exceptions are gradually increasing in number. The exceptions, however, trigger severe reactions, such as the election of a white male racist and sexist president to follow President Obama.

As I explain in the next chapter, there was never a scientific basis for "race." But the general public has usually been kept ignorant of this science.

The idea of "race" remains a fallacy today, just as it was a fallacy when used to justify slavery. We reinforce this fallacy every time we classify people as "white," "Black," "Asian," "Hispanic," "Native American" or whatever (whether with or without capital letters). These anti-scientific classifications impede our connecting to one another through recognition of our shared values, common interests, and common oppression.

At the same time, we cannot abandon these "racial" terms altogether, for they describe the false categorizations that have persisted for four centuries and continue to shape the lives of everyone. They affect where we live, whom we regularly associate with, whom we marry, what medical treatment we receive, the jobs that we have, and the distribution of power.

There is a reality to these false classifications, a reality created by society for the purpose of maintaining a hierarchical structure that benefits those at the top. This societal reality is like the reality of a mad person, real to the mad person but to no one else. But it is we who are mad. It is this madness — including the madness of slavery — that created "races." This societal idea of "race" is necessary to sustain the idea of "white" people. Sustaining the idea of a "white race" is the foundation of racism.

To progress beyond this societal madness, we must acknowledge the accepted existence of these false categories as we refuse to confirm them. Accordingly, I have chosen to place all "racial" terms in quotation marks. The quotation marks mean "so-called" — so-called by society but otherwise not real. Not only are they not real; they are positively destructive.

I do not, however, put quotation marks around the term *white supremacy* or *white male supremacy*. White supremacy and white male supremacy are ideas. They do not designate a "race" but a false and destructive way of thinking and behaving.

Many confuse cultural ethnicity with "race." But there is no one-to-one correlation between ethnicity and "race." There is no biological connection between the two. For example, there is no one-to-one correlation between those who identify themselves with a "Black" culture and those who are called "Black" by social convention. The same applies to people called "white," "Asian," and so on. There are no monolithic "white," "Black," or "Asian" cultures or ethnicities that have a one-to-one correlation to the people called those terms. Those who insist on such a correlation are supporting false stereotypes.

In short, these "racial" terms have no reality other than what society thinks they have. These "racial" terms are an essential part of the politics of racism. Using them to fight racism also supports racism and is, thus, counterproductive.

We can begin to undermine this despicable politics by putting all "racial" terminology in quotation marks as I do here. (I first introduced this idea to the public in a Letter to the Editor published in the *Boston Globe* on June 3, 2012. I explain this more thoroughly in my book, *Overcoming the Lie of 'Race': A Personal, Philosophical, and Political Perspective*, where in Chapter 9 I also explain how to transform but not abandon affirmative action.)

As I explain below in this chapter, it would a tragic mistake to confuse what I am proposing with colorblindness. We cannot be blind to what society and history have done to us. But we do not have to succumb to these social forces. Putting "racial" terms in quotation marks is a way to emerge from our slavery-based past that created "races" and instead create the non-racist—and non-sexist—future that we and our children deserve.

How American History Has Been Distorted

Since the settling of the American colonies and continuing into the present, the story of America has been told by or under the supervision of a select group consisting mostly of "white" males. Mostly "white" males have dominated the school boards and selection of textbooks in public schools and those who teach. "White" males have dominated the writing of the history textbooks and the publishing companies that decide what to print. Any legal challenges to this setup would be heard, until quite recently, by "white" male judges who had "white" male teachers using textbooks written by "white" male authors. It should surprise no one that the story of America has featured "white" males, portrayed as morally upright and honorable people, for "white" males are telling the story of how a "great nation" was born and grew.

This biased history focuses on the contributions of "white" males and says little about others. It is a history that mostly excludes women and people not "white." It is history written and perpetrated by those who implicitly or explicitly have accepted the idea that "white" people, particularly "white" males, should rule America even when it meant brutally relocating or exterminating most of the indigenous population, enslaving others, militarily invading other countries and backing autocracies and dictatorships to control and exploit non-"white" nations, including other nations in this hemisphere as well as others around the world.

The laws discussed here seek to suppress any viewpoints that suggest that the "white" males who are honored in United States history, including the founders, were anything other than morally upright people who may have occasionally made unintended mistakes. In this history, the history that nearly all of us were taught in primary and secondary schools, there may be only an occasional mention of anyone who is "Black," Asian, indigenous, or female. The roles of laborers, slaves, and women are an occasional aside if mentioned at all. The fact that much of the United States was built by slaves and Chinese laborers is rarely if ever mentioned. The state laws at issue here seek to exclude such uncomfortable facts from the public schools.

The effect of such history is to portray a distorted view where those most honored are "white" males. The psychological effect on students is to boost the morale of "white" males and to raise doubts in the minds of others about the worth of their ancestors and about their own capabilities. If anyone asked a "Black" child, "What have Black people contributed to America?" the child may not have an answer based on the history taught in the classroom. What "Blacks" accomplished is often segregated into February, one-twelfth of the year, and during that month, most of the "Blacks" celebrated are those most admired by the "whites" on the school boards who ultimately determine who is hired and what textbooks are to be used. Women face a similar fate.

For example, in high school I learned a lot—in February—about Booker T. Washington and almost nothing about W. E. B. Du Bois, who, in my view, had a much greater long-term beneficial impact and was a progressive thinker. Admittedly I was in high school many decades ago, but I cannot say that much has changed, particularly in conservative states. "Black" history is still segregated into February and often bland. There is even segregation in universities — including many elite ones — where African-American history, women's history, and indigenous American history are often confined to academic departments separated from the rest so as not to pollute them. These are examples of today's nationwide Jim Crow of the mind.

More recent history has also been distorted by the suppression of the contributions of women and people not "white." For example, the initial and lasting heroes of America's space adventures were the "white" males who rode the spaceships. But the mathematics that made their trips possible required the behind-the-scenes work of "Black" women mathematicians. Their vital contributions were suppressed for over fifty years until Margot Lee Shetterly, a "Black" woman scholar, made them known to the world.

The 1619 Project, first published in the *New York Times Magazine* in August, 2019, and now a book by that name, is a recent example of a direct critique of this biased history. Those states attempting to thwart this Project, by calling it "critical race theory" and banning anything that might be thought to be associated with it, have accepted the idea of white male supremacy, consciously or unconsciously, and are fighting to preserve it.

The book, *The 1619 Project,* contains some of the unpleasant history of America. This well-documented history conflicts with the idea that "white" males created a supposedly free and great nation. As a consequence of publishing this history, one of the people most responsible for *The 1619 Project,* Professor Nikole Hannah-Jones, was treated so disrespectfully by the Board of Trustees of the University of North Carolina that she decided to leave that institution. Some of the state laws examined here are designed to prevent any discussion of *The 1619 Project* and any other writings or ideas that might question that the role of "white" men praised in American history was other than honorable. These laws seek to suppress information about the contributions of non-"whites" or women to the development of the United States, or information that expose their oppression.

In short, American history as most of us know it assumes the idea of white male supremacy. The new state laws seek to preserve it.

How We Can Connect to One Another Based on Common Values, not "Race"

This book is not about any particular person's "race" but about ideas and values. On the one hand, not all "white" males accept the idea of white male supremacy, and on the other, many women, consciously or unconsciously, accept the idea of male supremacy. Many people not "white," consciously or unconsciously, accept the idea of white supremacy. This can be seen from the voting patterns of different groups.

Thus, when I speak of "white male supremacy," I am speaking about a way of thinking, often tacit and not fully conscious, and the behaviors that flow from it. I reject the idea that all "white" males are responsible for this way of thinking and behaving. What individuals think and do are not determined by "racial" designations. The people who are responsible for the laws addressed here are the legislators and officials who wrote, voted for, and enacted these laws, and their funders and supporters. Due to permitted campaign financing, the most influential of these supporters are wealthy elites who fund the candidates. Although most of those responsible are "white" males, there are also "Blacks" and women who join them.

The issue, then, is not about people's "races" or genders but about their values. An individual's values cannot be accurately identified by knowing that person's "race" and gender.

It is a sad and dangerous fact that many of the oppressed identify with their oppressors or unwittingly accept the very ideas and terminology that are the tools of oppression. Some "people of color" have implicitly adopted a white supremacist point of view and opposed those who have challenged the status quo, just as many women have implicitly adopted an anti-feminist point of view and have promoted a submissive role and urged other women to do the same. Some of the strongest supporters of views advanced by white male supremacists are a handful of influential "Black" male entertainers and politicians. "Black" police can be racist against other "Blacks." Some of the most vocal opponents of women's equality and their right to choose are women.

So it would be an horrendous error to assume that all "white" people accept the idea of white supremacy or that all men accept the idea of male supremacy. Even in slavery times, some slave masters wanted to free their slaves but could not, because more powerful slave masters wrote the laws that prevented it. Those who have written the laws typically have been funded by and have represented a powerful and wealthy minority. We cannot validly assume that a majority supported their views, for the majority most often was not in control or their views even known.

It is hopeful that many "white" males reject the idea of white male supremacy. Based on voting patterns, it is evident that nearly two-thirds of "white" male voters nationwide support white supremist candidates. The remainder who reject the idea of white male supremacy are a critical minority component of the majority of the people who oppose such candidates. But in the United States, due to its voter suppression laws, gerrymandering, and the Electoral College, a majority is not enough to win elections. A super-majority is needed.

The appropriate response to white male supremacy and the state and federal laws supporting it is for "white" women and men who oppose white male supremacy, and all people who are not "whites," to join together to repeal these laws. This joining of minorities, if sufficiently united, would create the super-majority that is needed.

The possibility of this happening is frightening to those who back these Jim-Crow-of-the-mind and anti-abortion state laws. They are a minority fighting to preserve their positions of power. This is why they want to ban discussion of such matters. They will do what they can to keep the society divided by gender and "race" and fund candidates who create and support these laws designed to keep this minority in control.

The false idea of "race" divides this potential super-majority into "racial" silos. But by focusing on our common values, not our "races," building this super-majority can be done. The women and men seen as inferior, consciously or unconsciously, by the supporters of white male supremacy, along with "white" males who deny their own superiority, have a common cause: building a society that is based on our equality and that voids the idea of white male supremacy.

It is our common values that can unite us and form a super-majority. "Race" and gender must not divide us.

Why "Colorblindness" Is an Error

It is assumed by many that the problem would be solved if we became "colorblind." This would mean that we ignore our "racial" differences. But to ignore our "racial" differences is to pretend that the ingrained racism of our society does not exist and has had no significant impact on our lives. Racism does not go away by ignoring it.

Instead of colorblindness, we need nonjudgmental color awareness and self-awareness, the awareness of how our society's classifications of us by "race" have impacted each of us. Nonjudgmental awareness means that we do not view our differences as criticism of the other or hostility towards the other but as awareness of the other and of ourselves. Friendships across "racial" lines, for example, would remain superficial without this nonjudgmental awareness. Such friendships would deepen if each seeks to become more self-aware and supportive of each other's awareness.

Similarly, men who wish to form close friendships with women will develop an empathetic awareness of the magnitude of women's oppression.

"Grandmother drowned herself in the river when she heard that grand-pap was going away."

— Mary James, a former slave
recounting in 1937 what happened
when her grandfather, a slave, was to be sold:
as quoted in "The harshest affliction,"
The Economist, June 18, 2022

CHAPTER 2

Jim Crow and Its Continuing False "Racial" Foundation

We cannot understand the racism of the present without an understanding of the racism of the past. What has been called *Jim Crow* is an essential part of that past. Jim Crow is still strong today; but it is often underground, unconscious, or indirect. The historical impact of Jim Crow openly surfaced when a mob led by white supremacists violently attacked the U.S. Capitol on January 6, 2021.

Jim Crow is about the many decades of "racial" segregation in the United States that followed the end of slavery and the Civil War. However, calling it "segregation" as it is usually termed glosses over the reality. That term implies only separation. Instead, it was about systematic oppression based on "race."

The Jim Crow period does not have a definite start or end date. It emerged gradually after the end of the Civil War. It was firmly established well before the twentieth century began. It was entrenched throughout most of the nation by the early twentieth century.

In the South, Jim Crow was fully defined by laws. It was nothing less than legalized apartheid. In the North, "racial" separation was the societal norm and firmly enforced by businesses and financial institutions whose practices were supported indirectly by laws that protected property rights. Whether by law or custom, Jim Crow was the dominant way of the United States.

Until 1954, when the United States Supreme Court decided *Brown* v. *Board of Education*, the Court had made it quite clear that separation of races was generally acceptable. In the 1896 case of *Plessy* v. *Ferguson*, the U.S. Supreme Court ratified "separate but equal" segregation of the "races," but the "equal" part of that phrase was an absurdity, as any observer knew. Prior to 1954, it was the U.S. Supreme Court's interpretations of the U.S. Constitution that allowed for and encouraged the white supremacist segregation laws that dominated more than the first half of the twentieth century.

This situation, generally from the late 1800's to years after 1954, was, as C. Vann Woodward described it in *The Strange Career of Jim Crow*, "a racial ostracism that extended to churches and schools, to housing and jobs, to eating and drinking. Whether by law or by custom, that ostracism eventually extended to virtually all forms of public transportation, to sports and recreations, to hospitals, orphanages, prisons, and asylums, and ultimately to funeral homes, morgues, and cemeteries."

I was personally subjected to a northern version of Jim Crow. I grew up in a segregated "Black" community in Kansas City, Kansas. In two different cities in Kansas, I was denied service in the late 1950's at a lunch counter and a restaurant. Kansas was an anti-slavery state, but Jim Crow was widespread.

Jim Crow was legal, but in the South it was often enforced illegally and lethally. Terry H. Anderson described Jim Crow's brutality: "Concerning race, the South was lawless. Whites owned the law, police, courts, press, and government. If a black brought charges against a white, it demonstrated disrespect to the superior race." In *The Souls of Black Folk*, published in 1903, W. E. B. Du Bois described it in the South, where there "grew up a double system of justice, which erred on the white side by undue leniency and the practical immunity of red-handed criminals, and erred on the black side by undue severity, injustice, and lack of discrimination. . . . It was not then a question of crime, but rather one of color, that settled a man's conviction on almost any charge." Until 1965, most "Black" people in the South could not vote due mostly either to racist enforcement of literacy tests and imposition of poll taxes or to violence.

Jim Crow was enforced with lynching by racist mobs. From the late nineteenth century well into the twentieth, American presidents did not speak out against it. The courts generally either ignored lynching or accepted it. President Theodore Roosevelt approved of it when the "Black" victim of lynching was accused of rape of a "white" woman — whether the accusation was proven or not.

Jim Crow did not emerge out of the blue. It was the historical product of the slavery that began in the colonies with the arrival of Africans in 1619. This long legacy of slavery overpowered the relatively brief period of partially liberalized "racial" relations during the decade that followed the Civil War. This legacy regarded those with African ancestry as mentally and morally inferior to "whites." It grew and became ingrained in the national culture prior to the Civil War and continued after it. This culturally ingrained view of "Blacks" meant that if the nation could not have slavery, it could at least enslave them culturally, educationally, politically and economically through segregation backed by the violence of lynchings and anti-"Black" urban riots that destroyed "Black" businesses and murdered people in "Black" communities. That is what Jim Crow meant to the nation that embraced it, North and South.

Jim Crow's physical oppression of those with African ancestry was always accompanied by mental oppression.

Slaves could not be allowed to reveal that they were as intelligent as Europeans, so their minds had to be enslaved as well as their bodies. Laws were enacted by the elites in power to prohibit teaching slaves to read and write. Even for a few years after the 1954 Supreme Court decision of *Brown* v. *Board of Education*, most state universities throughout the South did not allow "Black" students to enter. Barring "Black" students from higher education was also practiced earlier by some colleges in the North. W. E. B. Du Bois reported that Vassar College in the late nineteenth century would not (knowingly) admit "Negroes." In 1909, the president of Princeton University, Woodrow Wilson, who later became president of the United States, stated, "It is altogether inadvisable for a colored man to enter Princeton."

Barring "Blacks" from colleges meant suffocating any aspirations they might have had to develop their minds to the fullest and to compete for the best professional jobs. The barrier at the top rippled down to the bottom. Aspiring "Blacks" who wanted to be teachers could be diverted to less-reputable colleges, and with less-reputable degrees be limited to lesser-paying teaching jobs. That meant less money available in segregated "Black" communities. Thus, stifling the mind supported economic oppression as well.

My paternal grandfather, who was the principal of the segregated "Black" high school in Kansas City, Kansas for over three decades and had a bachelor's degree from the University of Indiana, fought against any attempt to stifle the minds of "Black" students. For his efforts, he was paid less than "white" principals—who had much less experience and similar or lesser college degrees—until a few months before his retirement in the early 1950's. He earned enough to not be poor and own his own home (which I grew up in), but nonetheless he was an economic victim of Jim Crow. Also, his lower salary meant that he had less money to spend in the community.

Brown v. *Board of Education* was the most significant of the U.S. Supreme Court decisions that slowly began to dismantle the Jim Crow laws that the Supreme Court itself had previously upheld. Ten years later, Congress passed the Civil Acts Act of 1964 that made it illegal to discriminate in public facilities and in employment. This was followed by the Voting Rights Act of 1965, which removed most of the racist barriers to voting. Jim Crow laws were not fully disabled, however, until 1967 when in *Loving* v. *Virginia* the U.S. Supreme Court ruled that states could not enforce laws against interracial marriages. What is remarkable is that one hundred and two years after the Civil War, many states in the North and South still had such laws and the government of Virginia openly defended them in front of the Supreme Court. Such laws determined your ancestry.

It was not until 1972 that the Civil Rights Act of 1964 was amended to prevent racist employment practices by state and local governments. That amendment enabled me to file a lawsuit against the State of California when I was denied tenure at California State University, East Bay (its current name) in 1974. As a result of the state's settling of that case, I received tenure in 1978. Thus, I was still fighting Jim Crow practices in the mid-to-late 1970's and would have failed without the new laws.

The embedded practices of centuries were not so easily abolished by Supreme Court decisions or new laws. Schools all over the country remained *de facto* segregated; home ownership for "Blacks" was often limited by banks and mortgage companies to areas that were already predominantly "Black" or by denying mortgages altogether. The culturally embedded idea of polarized "white" and "Black" "races" has remained, a polarization reinforced by the terminology of color opposites.

In most of the South, states still celebrate the Confederacy with holidays and monuments honoring those who fought to preserve slavery, thereby exalting what was a brutal, inhumane society and dishonoring those who suffered from it. These racist practices are what developed and have continued for over four hundred years following the arrival of Africans in America.

The cruel effects of Jim Crow never ended. These effects continued, for example, in police practices that frequently killed unarmed "Black" men. This is the lynching of today.

Less dramatic but more lethal has been the practice of medicine. Until 2021, in a liberal northern city known for quality health care, my health care provider over decades had two different categories for evaluating my kidney function based on the "estimated glomerular filtration rate." One category was used for "African Americans" and another category for everyone else. The mental functioning of "Black" football players was often assessed differently from the mental functioning of "white" football players, leaving more "Black" football players with undiagnosed brain damage, because it was assumed that lower mental functioning was normal for "Blacks." There is still a medicine, called "BiDil," which is prescribed only for "Blacks" without scientific evidence that "Blacks" benefit from it more than less-expensive alternatives available to others.

These are only a few examples of Jim Crow's continuing effects on the practice of medicine in America. The practice of medicine is supposed to be based in science, but there is no scientific basis for racially-based medicine. Instead, racially-based medicine is a political idea that reinforces the false belief (often unconscious) that "races" are biologically separate. The overall effect of this practice has often resulted in "Blacks" receiving inferior medical care or none.

The development of Jim Crow and its persistent effects could not have occurred without an earlier persuasive rationale for slavery. Slavery from its beginning was very controversial. Since many "white" people objected to slavery, a persuasive reason for it was needed to convince most people of its soundness.

That need became particularly critical after 1772, the year of a court decision in England, *Somerset* v. *Stewart*, which was interpreted by the English public to end slavery in England. This was four years before the Declaration of Independence. The supporters of slavery in Britain's American colonies feared that the impact of *Somerset* would eventually lead to the abolition of slavery in all of Britain's colonies, including theirs. This is why the southern colonies, whose economies were totally or almost totally dependent on slavery, joined the war of independence to divorce themselves from British rule. Their support for independence combined with that of the northern colonies made the 1776 Declaration of Independence a viable historical document leading to victory instead of a mere ranting of little lasting significance. Independence would preserve slavery—and it did, for Britain ended slavery in nearly all of its colonies more than thirty years before the ratification of the Thirteenth Amendment following the Civil War. Slaves would have been better off if the American Revolution had not occurred. Many slaves, knowing this, escaped to fight for the British. The northern colonies gladly accepted the southern colonies as partners in the fight against the British, making the northern colonies accomplices in the preservation of slavery.

The rationale for slavery that took hold was the idea that people were biologically divided into separate "races." This allowed for the idea that a biologically superior "white" race existed and that all other races were inferior, more animal-like than human. This idea became ingrained in the national fabric (and in much of Europe as well). In the states whose economies depended upon slavery, laws were developed to define those with African ancestry as the property of their owners. They were not people at all.

This point of view was formalized by the United States Supreme Court prior to the Civil War. It ruled in its 1857 decision of *Dred Scott* v. *Sandford*, "The right of property in a slave is distinctly and expressly affirmed in the Constitution." The Fifth Amendment of the Constitution, a part of the so-called Bill of Rights, was often relied upon during those times as protecting this right. The Fifth Amendment was incorporated into the constitutional protection of the right of slave owners to treat slaves as their property, no different from a horse or a pig. The slaves themselves had no constitutional rights whatsoever. They were property, not people.

The *Dred Scott* decision also summed up the national as well as the European acceptance of racist ideology (though in Europe, slaves did not become property and retained their status as people):

> It is difficult at this day to realize the state of public opinion in relation to that unfortunate race which prevailed in the civilized and enlightened portions of the world at the time of the Declaration of Independence and when the Constitution of the United States was framed and adopted. But the public history of every European nation displays it in a manner too plain to be mistaken.
>
> They had for more than a century before been regarded as beings of an inferior order, and altogether unfit to associate with the white race either in social or political relations, and so far inferior that they had no rights which the white man was bound to respect, and that the negro might justly and lawfully be reduced to

slavery for his benefit. He was bought and sold, and treated as an ordinary article of merchandise and traffic whenever a profit could be made by it. This opinion was at that time fixed and universal in the civilized portion of the white race. It was regarded as an axiom in morals as well as in politics which no one thought of disputing or supposed to be open to dispute, and men in every grade and position in society daily and habitually acted upon it in their private pursuits, as well as in matters of public concern, without doubting for a moment the correctness of this opinion.

—Quoted from *Dred Scott* v. *Sandford*, 60 U.S. 393, 407 (1857).

Not all "white" people, however, agreed with this opinion. Nine years later, at the end of the Civil War, "white" men ratified the Thirteenth Amendment which abolished slavery. But the views expressed in the *Dred Scott* opinion were nonetheless a prevalent sentiment throughout the nation. For over one hundred years after the *Dred Scott* decision, nearly all U.S. presidents expressed a white supremacist point of view, as I documented in my book, *Presidential Racism*. Today, white supremacist views still threaten to destroy many decades of national progress.

Jim Crow, thus, did not emerge as an anomaly in U.S. history. Instead, it emerged from a cultural foundation that had been centuries in the making. The essential cement that has held this foundation together is the idea of "race." This ingrained idea still governs behavior throughout the nation and, mostly due to centuries of European colonialism, has been spread around much of the world. It is an idea that helps separate people hierarchically into competing factions, enables ethnic cleansing and genocide, suffocates friendships and love across fictitious boundaries, and is a frequent rationale for violence, oppression, and the undermining of the values of democracy.

The idea of classifying people into "races," as that term is understood today, does not have a clear origin. The idea of human "races" appeared in 1684 in a French anthropological journal, but it attracted little notice. The idea was more widely noticed when proposed by a well-known Swedish scientist, Carl Linnaeus, in 1738, and later others developed and promoted the idea, notably Buffon in 1749, but these earlier ideas were not explicitly given as justifications for slavery or oppression. The hierarchical classification and oppression of people based on their apparent ancestry was not due to them but had begun much earlier in the colonies.

The term "mulatto" appeared in Virginia records in 1666. Two years earlier, Maryland had enacted a law that punished English women who married "Negroes" — the men were not punished. In 1679 a Massachusetts court record referred to a "mulatto" slave. Throughout many of the colonies, beginning in the mid-seventeenth century, classifications of people as Africans, "mulattos" and other mixtures involving the indigenous peoples were used to justify their oppression and enslavement. Many laws of the colonies as well as social practices lumped these mixtures together with Africans as slaves or as those who could become slaves.

These laws reflected the false idea that the English were somehow pure and that mixtures were not pure. This merged into the idea of "white" people, people who were pure and unmixed with others of darker skin. The mixed children of these "white" people were not pure and therefore could not be "white." The impure with African ancestry and partial African ancestry became "Negroes," "mulattoes," and later simply "Blacks," names that completely separated them from the supposed purity of "whites."

The creation of polarized opposites, "Black" and "white," obscured the uncomfortable fact that many of the children of slaves had "white" fathers—and sometimes mothers. That some of these people of mixed ancestry were often regarded as "white" because they looked "white" was a contradiction that was overlooked then as now. Today, we continue this absurdity by talking about an "interracial" marriage as though the "races" are separate and only newly joined in an infrequent marriage.

The early classifications and social practices in the colonies provided the cultural foundation for the development of the idea of "race." Once this different treatment of people became the norm of society and incorporated into laws, it was only a small step to accept the idea that the difference of ancestry was a product of biological "races" that had developed separately from the beginning of human life.

As Jacques Barzun demonstrated in *Race: A Study in Superstition*, first published in 1937, there was never any sound reasoning to support the idea of "race." It was simply an idea that fit with societal practice and laws, so it was convenient to believe it, for it could be used to assure the public that the society's hierarchical structure was an unchangeable product of nature or created by God.

By the time Charles Darwin reported empirical evidence obtained from his voyages around the world, the idea of "race," invented from the armchair, was so firmly established and politically useful that his evidence was largely ignored. In *The Descent of Man*, published in 1871, Darwin said that differences among people that he observed around the world did not correlate to the accepted idea of "race," and he called the idea of distinct human "races" "extremely improbable." In the twentieth century, all evidence located the origin of the human species in Africa, with no evidence of "races" that developed from different origins. More recently, evidence based on DNA analysis has confirmed that different early human types — incorrectly defined as separate species — intermingled and had viable children.

Thus, the idea of a "pure race" is contradicted by these mixtures among different types of humans that began hundreds of thousands of years ago. Even the earlier idea that *Homo sapiens* is a separate and pure species is contradicted by such evidence. It follows that "white" people cannot be a pure "race" but instead are the product of different human groups and types intermingling, having viable children, and evolving with different skin coloring over thousands of years to become more compatible with the climate. The same is true for all people falsely considered to be a "race."

Furthermore, the intermingling of different human groups has continued throughout human history. I summarized numerous examples of it in Chapters 4, 5, and 6 of *Overcoming the Lie of "Race."* There are, of course, observable variations from one human group to another; but genetically these variations are small and do not correlate to the current and historic usage of the word "race." Instead of a sharply defined separation of one group from another, the groups are linked by continuums that bridge any imagined gaps.

The mixture of different human groups is the norm in human history. It did not take long for "mulattos" to be born after the arrival of Africans in 1619. Some of these mixtures had very light skins and were regarded as "white," and they in turn mixed with other people called "white." The widespread African and indigenous people's partial ancestry of "white" people in the United States is a confirmed fact that has been suppressed. Even many of the English people who first arrived on American soil likely carried African genes from Roman armies around two thousand years ago, for many members of those Roman armies were African, and many of those soldiers stayed in England and married English women after the armies retreated. These historical facts in themselves expose the lie of "race" and destroy the very idea of a pure "white" people.

Scientific studies have confirmed the non-existence of biological "races." As early as 1937, analysis of human genes confirmed that there are no indivisible "racial" clusters of genes. For example, there is no biological connection between skin color and intelligence. Based on this and other empirical data, anthropologist Ashley Montagu wrote *Man's Most Dangerous Myth: The Fallacy of Race*, originally published in 1942. Since then, further analysis of the genetic makeup of humans has confirmed that the idea of biological "races" is a fallacy. In 2018, the *American Journal of Human Genetics* summed up the empirical findings of decades: "Genetics demonstrates that humans cannot be divided into biologically distinct subcategories. . . . This is validated by many decades of research. . . . Genetics exposes the concept of 'racial purity' as scientifically meaningless."

Thus, biologically distinct "races" do not exist. The word "race" should be dropped for our language when referring to any human group. "Races" exist only as a false idea in the minds of those who believe that they exist. Unfortunately this false belief pervades the entire society.

The social structure of the United States is founded on this false idea. It is founded on a lie. The lie of biological "races" resulted in the political creation of separate "racial" groups within the society. Mixtures have been stuffed into separate non-"white" "racial" categories, guided or forced into separate living quarters, at first enslaved and later denied economic opportunities available to "whites" — all based on "race" to hide the fact of their mixtures and to sustain a hierarchically structured society that calls itself a democracy based on the idea of human equality. This contradictory absurdity is an impenetrable barrier to creating a healthy democracy.

A healthy society does not abandon science in favor of myths and lies. Widespread confirmed evidence is the anchor of societal sanity. Such evidence establishes that "races" as we understand them today simply do not biologically exist.

In short, the idea of "race" was concocted to support the idea of white supremacy and slavery. "Race" is not biological but is a political and social creation that pervades our society and enables racism.

To maintain "racial" distinctions, the idea of "race" is called a "social construct" by many of those who recognize that "race" is not biological. As a social construct, the idea of "race" is a reality. But the social construct was concocted to rationalize slavery, colonialism, and racism. Its function today is to maintain the idea of a "white" race, an idea that is necessary to make white supremacy possible.

Do we want to perpetuate this social construct? We perpetuate it whenever we call people "white," "Black," "Asian," and other terms thought to be descriptions of someone's "race," unless we qualify such terms with quotation marks or by other effective means. By using quotation marks, we acknowledge the reality of the social construct but do not affirm the validity of this construct.

Throughout human history in much of the world there has been slavery or its equivalent. Ancient Greece and ancient Rome, for example, contained slaves and mistreated women; therefore, they provide no model for today. Many "race"-like ideas have been used to justify slavery and aristocracy, ideas asserting that ancestry or blood-lines determine superiority or inferiority. What we call "races" today is just another version of these age-old rationales. These rationales viciously combat the idea of human equality. They also devalue our individuality. As individuals—of equal worth with other individuals—we are who we are regardless of how society classifies us.

The idea of "race" also affects our sense of ourselves, for many find their identity in defining themselves as belonging to one "race" or another. This group identification opens the door to and even encourages a closed or insular view of identity. Such a view emphasizes separateness from others of a different "race" or group, usually accompanied by a sense of the moral or biological superiority of one's own group. Insular identity creates an identity closed circle where empathy is confined within the circle and is thwarted, often by hostility, for those outside of the circle.

Although group identity is often insular in this way, it does not have to be. There is little harm if ethnic or other group identity is not insular but open. Open identity acknowledges how one may have been affected by one's cultural environment that differs from the cultural environment of others, but such acknowledgement is accompanied by a strong sense of our common humanity that connects us regardless of these cultural differences. Open identity means that empathy with those of different identities is the same as with those of the same identity.

In our society, however, "racial" identity is too often closed and insular, not open. Closed, insular "racial" identity was necessary to support slavery and Jim Crow, and that view of identity has been ingrained in American culture for nearly four hundred years, accepted by the victims as well as by the victimizers.

Since the idea of "race" was concocted as a biological idea, most people still think or assume, often unconsciously, that there is some biological basis for it. The resistance to accepting empirical data that refutes the idea of biologically based "races" is a curious social phenomenon. Myth has conquered fact. Lies have conquered science.

The myths and lies of "race" are not confined to any one nation or region. The massacre of six million Jews in the Holocaust resulted from these myths and lies. The Nazis' racist laws used the United States' Jim Crow laws as their models, linking these two historical tragedies. Ethnic cleansings in parts of Europe and elsewhere throughout the world have been and continue to be the outcome of myths and lies that people hold on to in the face of empirical data that contradicts their ingrained beliefs.

Why do we deny science in favor of myths and lies?

It is a question that has not been answered. Finding the answer could transform the world we live in, replacing war with peace.

The state laws examined here seek to suppress any discussion of this *Why?* In these states, in-depth examination of racism and sexism must not be allowed. The laws require continued living in the realm of culturally ingrained myths and lies that must not be questioned. These laws mean that empirical studies and data are not just irrelevant but the enemy.

But we must seek answers to this *Why?* Why do myths and lies conquer confirmed evidence and science? It is not enough to say that the truth will ultimately prevail, because myths and lies kill people while the submerged truth awaits its day to emerge. Today's myths and lies about "race" set the stage for the next Holocaust or worse.

We must strenuously oppose the perpetuation of the state laws examined here, for they forbid in-depth discussion of racism and sexism. We also must inquire into the bizarre but widespread mentality that led to these laws, the mentality that replaces empirical inquiry with fiction designed to prevent empirical inquiry. It is an anti-scientific mentality, one that has plagued humankind throughout its history. These laws stifle inquiry and thereby delay the emergence of truth and may cause truth to remain submerged while we hate and kill one another due to lies, myths, and superstition.

"No oppressive order could permit the oppressed to begin to question: Why?"
— Paulo Freire, *Pedagogy of the Oppressed*

"All slaveholders agreed that the thinking slave was a potentially rebellious slave."
— Richard Kluger, *Simple Justice:
The History of* Brown *v.* Board of Education
and Black America's Struggle for Equality

CHAPTER 3

Beyond Legality

In Montana, the Superintendent of Public Instruction asked the Attorney General for a legal opinion on the legality of teaching "critical race theory" and anti-racism in the public schools. Attorney General Austin Knudsen issued his opinion, dated May 27, 2021. Essentially his opinion is not only an attempted legal defense of any state laws that would ban "critical race theory" from public schools. It is also a philosophical attack on the ideas he believes are contained in "critical race theory."

As a legal opinion, it is flawed, as I will explain. As a philosophical attack on "critical race theory," it does not belong in a legal opinion and blends the writer's own philosophical point of view with his view of the legality of certain actions and expressions.

More fundamentally, the very request for a legal opinion and its issuance assumes an answer to a question that must be addressed: Is the law of the nation free from racism and sexism? A legal opinion cannot address that question.

Consider, for example, a legal opinion that could have been issued in 1860 concerning the legality of slavery in the United States. Based on the U.S. Supreme Court decision, *Dred Scott* v. *Sanford* (1857), the answer would have been that slavery was legal.

Consider, for example, a legal opinion that could have been issued in 1945 concerning the legality of racial segregation in the United States. Citing the U.S. Supreme

Court decision of *Plessy* v. *Ferguson* (1896), the answer would have been that racial segregation was legal.

Consider, for example, a legal opinion that could have been issued in 1918 concerning whether women had a constitutional right to vote. The answer would have been that they did not.

Consider, for example, a legal opinion that could have been issued in 1965 concerning whether a state could ban "interracial" marriages. In many states, such as Virginia, the answer would have been that it could.

Consider, for example, a legal opinion that could be issued in 2023 concerning whether a state may have laws that impose criminal sanctions on any woman who has an abortion. Citing the U.S. Supreme Court decision, *Dobbs* v. *Jackson Women's Health Organization* (2022), the answer would be that it can.

The *Dobbs* decision indicates that sexism is indeed embedded in the laws of the nation. The state laws examined here, along with many other state laws that disproportionately suppress the ability to vote in predominantly "Black" neighborhoods, indicate that racism is indeed embedded in the laws of the nation.

If we think a legal opinion can determine whether an ideal or practice is racist or sexist, we assume that the laws of the nation are free of racism and sexism. To make that assumption is to beg the question: Are the nation's laws free of racism and sexism? That is a question that must be examined with appeals to a higher standard that is not based in law.

What is that standard?

The standard that I use is based on the ideas of human equality and the golden rule. I interpret these ideas to mean that every human being is of equal worth. I explained my views in my book, *How We Are Our Enemy – And How to Stop: Our Unfinished Task of Fulfilling the Values of Democracy*,

Chapter 6, and I elaborated further in my essay, "The Enduring Anti-Democratic Disease Afflicting Us—And Its Cure," contained in Part I of my book, *Presidential Racism: The Words of U.S. Presidents Since the Civil War*.

These views are my bias. My bias is shared with a multitude of others. I do not claim that my bias is due to Nature or God. I think of it as the most reasonable way for all to live. I cannot prove it absolutely. I can only seek to persuade others who are unsure or do not fully agree.

To his credit, Attorney General Austin Knudsen also appeals to a higher standard, the concept that "all men are created equal." But he misinterprets that standard to mean that everyone must be *treated* equally. He often relies on concurring opinions of Supreme Court Justices and mistakenly presents these minority opinions as the law of the land.

But more importantly, *equal worth and equal treatment are not the same*. To value the equal worth of a person who is poor does not mean that the poor should be taxed in exactly the same way as the rich are taxed. To value the equal worth of a person who has a physical disability means to provide physical accommodations for that person that are not provided to others who do not have that disability. To value the equal worth of those who are the victims of a disaster means to provide them with medical care and other forms of assistance that need not be given to others. To value the equal worth of women does not mean passing a law that prohibits abortions worded so that it could equally apply to men. Equal treatment not only is not the same as equal worth. Equal treatment can in some situations—such as taxing everyone equally—be contrary to equal worth.

These are the fundamental fatal flaws of Knudsen's legal opinion. There are additional flaws as well which I address separately in the next chapter and in Chapter 17.

I do not address in this book the merits or demerits of various ideas proposed by those called proponents of "critical race theory." I do propose an ethical standard of equal worth for discussing these matters. We cannot fruitfully discuss these ideas by banning them from the public schools.

"Totalitarianism is not simply amoral. It is the morality of the closed society — of the group, or of the tribe; it is not individual selfishness, but it is collective selfishness."
— Karl R. Popper, *The Open Society and its Enemies*

CHAPTER 4

Components of Jim Crow of the Mind

Each of the fifteen states examined here has enacted laws to ban meaningful discussion of racism or both racism and sexism in the public schools. They also ban any meaningful inquiry into the extent to which racism or sexism has permeated America throughout its history. Most of these laws specifically expel from the classroom exploration of unconscious racist or sexist assumptions.

These laws have been used as an excuse to ban books in the public schools and libraries, even though the laws themselves do not call for banning books from libraries.

Since the writers of these books are disproportionately "Black" or feminist, the laws establish a mental segregation separating the ideas that examine racism and sexism from the ideas that implicitly, tacitly, or openly accept or support the idea of white male supremacy. Like racial segregation of the past, this is not "separate but equal" but a vicious hierarchical separation that facilitates suppression of any view that challenges or criticizes the idea of white male supremacy.

What is the standard for judging these laws? In my view the goal should be to create an environment in the classroom where issues of racism, sexism, and other gender-related and group identification issues can be discussed while the equal worth of every student and the teacher is respected. Some supporters of these laws are trying to achieve that goal for students but are supporting laws that instead create a disrespectful environment for teachers and also adversely affect students who want to learn.

The laws suppress the discussion of history and the critical issues of the present and leave students in ignorance to learn about others from the street and their parents. The laws are typically vague and leave teachers without clear guidance about what can be said in the classroom and what cannot be said. As a result, teachers self-censor; for if they violate the law, they could be fired, sued, or their license to teach taken away. The laws that suppress the teaching of slavery, racism, and sexism in American history are themselves the product of mostly unconscious racism and sexism, which is why these laws often confine or bar discussion of unconscious beliefs.

The laws are designed to protect "white" male students from confronting their own privileges and from feeling discomfort when racism or sexism is discussed. This is why they are called laws against "critical race theory," which is mostly (but not exclusively) the product of "Black" academics and intellectuals who are seeking to understand and solve racism in America. There were previously no similar laws to protect "Black" students from discomfort. But most of these laws are also laws against feminism, for they lump racism and sexism together as subjects that can be discussed only in limited, superficial ways.

These laws frequently contain some or all of the following features.

1. Stifle Discussion of Unconscious Racism or Sexism

Without including unconscious behaviors and unconscious assumptions, discussion of racism or sexism is superficial and ultimately meaningless.

Summing up several studies, a columnist in *The Economist* stated, "The submerged part of the iceberg, implicit racial beliefs and associations, plays a bigger role than was once realized. Overcoming those is particularly difficult because of their semi-conscious nature." Racist assumptions, thus, exist at a level that is often beneath consciousness. It emerges in the way we use language.

For example, "Black" athletes who excel in team sports are often praised for their athletic ability but not for the intelligence that is required for their success. Such praise is misguided racism of which the writer is often not aware. This bias is so widespread that a computerized model can correctly predict whether athletes were "white" or "Black" from the language used to describe them.

Similarly, it is endemic that much focus on notable women is on what they are wearing. Such focus is on their bodies, diverting attention away from their intelligence and contributions.

Many of these state laws have the effect of barring discussion of unconscious racism and sexism. Yet, among people who are not consciously racist or sexist, their racism and sexism exist beneath their awareness. This results in behavior that can be insulting to people considered to be "Black," "Asian" or "Latino," or to women, while the perpetrator of the insult has no idea why an insult has occurred. Many unconscious insulters would change their behavior if they understood what they had done.

The state laws that bar or restrict discussion of this unconscious behavior do not want these issues explored. In effect, the laws protect the status quo and impede any progress towards overcoming racism, sexism, and other gender-related oppression.

These state laws are the products of a political ideology with the implicit—sometimes conscious but nearly always including the unconscious—assumption of white male supremacy.

2. Restrict Discussion of Controversial Issues, Sometimes Including Anything that Makes Others Feel Uncomfortable

It is not possible to avoid what is controversial, since it depends on the perspective of the perceiver. Even established facts can be controversial to those who reject them.

For me, for example, it is not controversial that vaccinations can reduce the frequency of certain diseases. This has been confirmed by innumerable studies over many decades. It is also confirmed by my personal experience with the vaccinations that protect against influenza.

But there is a small minority of people who reject all vaccinations. To them, vaccinations are controversial. They are the ones who make it controversial when it should not be.

Some state laws require teachers to be "objective" if controversial subjects come up in the classroom. For example, my view is that the only objective position is that which scientific studies support. However, a school administrator who opposes vaccinations (or in response to public pressure) would regard me, if I were a teacher, as not objective. To this administrator, being objective would probably mean giving equal weight to both sides. Since I would not give equal weight to those who oppose science, this administrator would regard me as biased. To avoid being seen as biased so that I could keep my job, I would have to avoid any discussion of the matter in the classroom.

As for the discussion of racism or sexism, avoiding discussion of it altogether is probably what the laws intend to accomplish. In any case, that will be the laws' effect.

The word "objective" is one of the most unobjective terms in the English language. Determining what is "objective" cannot be objectively defined. Where there is disagreement, the meaning of "objective" depends on the perspective of the person making the judgment. A requirement that teachers be "objective" means simply that objectivity is ultimately determined by those with the power to hire and fire teachers: the administrators and governing boards. Their biases determine the meaning of "objectivity" because of the power of their positions.

3. Name *The 1619 Project* as Objectionable

The 1619 Project was initially a collection of articles published by the *New York Times Magazine* in 2019. There is now a book of that title that significantly expands the Project. The thesis of the Project is that American history must give significant weight to the history of slavery that began in 1619 with the arrival of African slaves on the shores of the British colony of Virginia, and that understanding that history is essential to understanding American history and racism today.

The book contains well-documented studies that every American should know about. Suppressing discussion of the book or its views is to impose ignorance in the classroom, transforming schools into centers of political indoctrination that eschew learning and inquiry.

Some states specifically name in their laws or rules *The 1619 Project* as one of the subjects to be avoided in the classroom, or they ban discussion of ideas like those contained in *The 1619 Project*. Many others target "critical race theory," an undefined term that basically means any discussion of racism a "white" official or enforcer does not like.

As a practical matter, that means that views reflecting any content of *The 1619 Project* are also targets. Thus, it is not just *The 1619 Project* itself that is pronounced as objectionable, but by implication any of the content and ideas expressed in it.

Essentially these laws shut down any meaningful discussion about the role and impact of slavery in the United States. Such laws themselves are a product of slavery and its Jim Crow aftermath. Their very existence validates the fundamental idea of *The 1619 Project*.

4. Adopt the Arrogance of Objectivity

Montana Attorney General Austin Knudsen's legal opinion (discussed in the previous chapter) asserts that the traits of "'individualism,' 'hard work,' 'objectivity,' 'progress,' "politeness,' 'decision-making,' and 'delayed gratification'" are "self-evident virtues—universally applicable to and shared by people of all races, colors, creeds, and national origins" and "far from being hallmarks of merely 'white culture,' are in fact important hallmarks of a virtuous and productive colorblind society."

The assertion that these are self-evident virtues reflects a cultural bias of those in positions of power. For example, during the existence of slavery the master determined that "hard work" was an important trait of a good slave. To a slave, however, working hard for a cruel master was to support one's own oppression. This was not a virtue. It made more sense to do the minimum necessary to avoid beatings and do as lIttle as possible to support the master. Today, it is the employer who sees "hard work" as a virtue for the employees while the employer may be working hard too or vacationing in the Bahamas. Even so, periods of relaxation are usually essential to being productive and to enjoying your work—as long as the boss does not see you when you are relaxing or having fun.

"Objectivity" is a virtue for those in positions to determine what is objective and what is not. In past households—and in some present ones—it was the husband who determined when his wife was not being objective. When it comes to opinions and points of view, determining what is "objective" is a matter of economic and political power, for it is those with that power who decide what is objective and what is not. Males ("white" and non-"white") often assume this role over women. "Objective" history has mostly been written to chronicle empires and conquerors. Rarely does anyone attempt to write a history from the perspective of the victims or of the opponents of celebrated empires. The people historians call "barbarians" had civilizations too, sometimes ones that were peaceful unless attacked, but they are often not studied and have been prejudged by terminology. Unless we are dealing with facts established by observable evidence, or the abstractions of mathematics, objectivity is not objective.

To proclaim that the traits Mr. Knudsen lists are universal is to identify with those with the power to decide whether others conform to them. It is arrogant to claim that these are universally virtuous traits when others have questioned them. Traditionally in our society, "white" males in positions of power have the role of determining what is hard work and what is objectivity. Consciously or unconsciously, many "white" males have accepted that role. They presume to know the answer when others disagree. They will not consider whether their views are nothing more than a cultural bias, for they assume that they are the representatives of what is objective and universal.

Many of the state laws examined here allow discussion of controversial issues pertaining to racism and sexism but only as long as the teacher is objective and unbiased. But it is not the teacher who is given the authority to determine what is objective and unbiased. It is the teacher's employer. We should not overlook the fact that in the public schools the teachers are disproportionately women and the higher authorities in the educational hierarchies are usually disproportionately men.

5. Prohibit Discussing Whether Testing for "Merit" Has A Racially Discriminatory Impact

Many of the new state laws contain language that effectively prohibits discussion in a public school classroom whether the idea of "merit" or "meritocracy" has a discriminatory impact on "Blacks" or women. The problem with "merit" is that it is subject to cultural bias. Who defines "merit"? Who creates the means of testing for "merit"? These are questions that cannot be discussed in the classroom in many of these states.

I addressed these questions in Chapter 9 of my book *Overcoming the Lie of "Race."* For example, I stated:

> In higher education, the bias favoring "white" males—more specifically, upper-class and middle-class "white" males with well-educated parents—is the result of over-reliance on standardized test scores. As I will explain, test scores reflect on a certain kind of intelligence, a narrow kind that does not necessarily translate into accomplishments in the real world.

I also proposed another way of defining merit in determining admissions to higher education.

The states that bar discussion of this in the classroom do not want any questioning of the societal processes that may be biased in favor of "white" males.

6. Use Fuzzy Language and Rhetorical Tricks

These laws often contain key clauses that are unclearly written, so for many behaviors it is unclear whether the law applies. They may contain *wiggle words*, like "objective" and "patriotism," whose meanings wiggle because they depend on the perspectives of the speaker or the audience.

They also may contain *rubber band words or phrases* whose meanings can be contracted or stretched to be more restrictive or less restrictive, narrower or broader. For example, a word that frequently appears in these laws as something prohibited is to "inculcate." This word normally means to repeatedly and forcefully express an idea or a point of view that the speaker wants the listeners to accept. But how many times is required for it to be "repeatedly used" and how forceful does it have to be to qualify as inculcation? An anxious or overly vigilant parent or student could report a teacher's mere mention of a prohibited concept as an attempt to inculcate, and thereby put the teacher on the defensive. An overly strict enforcer of the law can construe the word broadly to intimidate a teacher. The teacher, on the other hand, may have had no warning that mentioning a concept two or three times might be construed as inculcating. That possibility would likely silence the teacher.

Another rubbery prohibited concept is the idea that a person's "race" or color can make that person "inherently racist." I agree that no one is inherently racist. But what if I raise for discussion the idea that racism is inherent in our society and causes everyone to think in racial terms, which is a primary cause of individual racism? Is this a prohibited concept that cannot be discussed? Nothing in the law would prevent an accuser or enforcer from thinking that my topic for discussion is a prohibited concept, even though that would stretch the law beyond its literal meaning. Since how this law is interpreted could determine a teacher's future, a teacher concerned about this would likely be silent. Most likely the idea would not be discussed.

The governing interpretations, of course, are in the hands of those who enforce these laws. The fuzzier or more stretchable the law, the more power the enforcers have. The accusers also have power to harass and may use that power to make even broader interpretations of the law than those of conscientious enforcers.

A frequently used rhetorical trick is to include lists of terms in the law connected by "or." Included in the list will be terms that nearly everyone would agree with; but also included are alternative terms, connected by "or," that are very controversial or even draconian. Politicians can then say that the law accomplishes what the agreeable terms mean and ignore the alternative terms that are controversial or draconian. But it is the alternative controversial and draconian terms that do the most damage.

For example, my imagined law could "prohibit public littering or gathering in groups of two or more." I would correctly promote the law as prohibiting littering. I would say nothing about gatherings.

You will see real examples in some of the state-by-state chapters.

7. Subject Teachers to Discipline for Not Complying with the Law

These state laws control what teachers teach in public school classrooms. The control is over the teachers' livelihoods, their salaries, and their jobs. For a teacher to be fired in one of these states or lose the credential to teach is likely to mean that the teacher will not be able to teach in any of the remaining states with similar laws. It is fear of such consequences that will control what happens in the classroom. Since the laws are often vague, it means that to be safe, a teacher must avoid any subject that might likely to be seen as discussing racism, sexism, and other gender-related issues. The result is not only control of what the teachers teach, but control of what students learn. Such control will make most of these students too uninformed to intelligently participate in the diverse world that awaits them upon their graduation.

8. Contribute to Cultural Vigilantism

Many of these states have websites that ask residents to report any teacher who might be violating these laws.

Although the laws themselves are vague, these websites are often vaguer. They allow a child to report to a parent things said by a public school teacher whom the child does not like. The parent may then fill out a report on the website. There is plenty of room for exaggeration, misinterpretation, misunderstanding and retribution. These websites, along with the statements of state officials, encourage vigilante behavior against teachers.

Vigilantes act on their own to punish those who are accused of doing something the vigilantes do not like. The punishment occurs outside of the framework of law. Public officials become vigilantes when they openly advocate punishment of others without due process of law. Vigilantes act as police, prosecutors, judges and executioners bundled into one.

Cultural vigilantism targets the expression of ideas for punishment. Any expression of ideas that deviates from an accepted norm is attacked along with those who express them. A typical form of cultural vigilantism is the banning of books and the firing of teachers who are thought to have expressed ideas like those contained in the books. When public officials call for the banning of books where no law authorizes the banning, they are not only vigilantes themselves, they are also arousing the public to be vigilantes too. In this way, vigilantism is officially sponsored.

Officially sanctioned vigilantism to enforce conformity is a common practice in China. Officially sponsored vigilantism enforced by the public is an effective form of totalitarianism. People spy on each other. Anyone who steps out of line is reported to the authorities. This kind of totalitarianism is now growing in the United States and is encouraged by these state laws.

The laws examined here are often cited by vigilante officials as the basis for their calls for suppression of ideas and expressions pertaining to racism, sexism, gay relationships, and women's right to choose. The laws themselves often do not authorize such widespread suppression, but the laws are usually vague with undefined terms that allow for interpretation beyond the literal wording of the laws. For example, the officials may call for the expulsion of "critical race theory" even when the laws do not mention that term. Since "critical race theory" is not clearly defined, it can mean whatever the officials want it to mean. They can claim that the vague laws are meant to suppress critical race theory—whether the laws mention the term or not.

Thus, cultural vigilantism will find offense in things that the law does not mention but which the law does not prohibit. Officials can lead the public to think that these laws require or support removing books from public libraries, even though these laws may explicitly contain no such requirement. When public officials name books that should be banned, they encourage other members of the public to act on their own, searching out the books, removing them from shelves and perhaps burning them.

The states that name *The 1619 Project* within their laws, rules, or statements of officials sanction the vigilante removal of the book with that title from any place where a student might find it—from libraries, bookstores, and from the hands of anyone reading it on the bus.

Similar vigilante action is encouraged against any book that an official names as offensive. Typically these are books which in varying degrees critically examine or expose tacit white male supremacy. (Other laws attack anything officials deem to be sexually deviant.)

The Combined Effect

These laws taken together encourage a new form of lynching—the strangling of minds. Minds are strangled by cutting off the information and views that they need to grow. Just as physical lynching underpinned Jim Crow, so does strangling of minds underpin Jim Crow of the mind.

Many of these laws contain a list of "prohibitive" concepts—concepts that are prohibited from the classroom. Since these laws themselves describe the prohibited concepts, the laws prohibit themselves from being discussed in the classroom, so that teachers cannot even discuss some of these laws in the classroom without violating them.

States with Harmless Laws Sometimes Billed as Against "Critical Race Theory"

In most of the states addressed in the following chapters, harmful laws are mixed in with provisions that I do not consider to be harmful. Three states have only the harmless provisions, though for political reasons they have sometimes been advertised as banning "critical race theory." These three states (as of this book's publication date) are Idaho, Mississippi, and Utah. I do not include these states in the following chapters, and I do not discuss the harmless provisions that are part of the laws of many of the states that also have harmful provisions.

Utah has four provisions, all of which I consider to be harmless. Idaho has three of the same provisions (though with somewhat different wording), and Mississippi has two of them worded differently.

Here are Utah's provisions, contained in the rules of the State Board of Education, R277-328-3:

> (3) The professional learning provided by an LEA may not include instruction that promotes or endorses that:
>
> (a) a student or educator's sex, race, religion, sexual orientation, gender identity or membership in any other protected class is inherently superior or inferior to another sex, race, religion, sexual orientation, gender identity or any other protected class;
>
> (b) a student or educator's sex, race, religion, sexual orientation, gender identity or membership in any other protected class determines the content of the student or educator's character including the student or educator's values, morals, or personal ethics;
>
> (c) a student or educator bears responsibility for the past actions of individuals from the same sex, race, religion, sexual orientation, gender identity or any other protected class as the student or educator; and
>
> (d) a student or educator should be discriminated against or receive adverse treatment because of the student or educator's sex, race, religion, sexual orientation, gender identity or membership in any other protected class.

I view these provisions, because they are not part of harmful provisions, as not preventing or stifling the discussion of racism and sexism in the classroom. If applied carefully, they even set the groundwork for discussing racism and sexism fruitfully.

The following chapters examine the extent to which the laws of a state contain harmful features, sometimes including others not described above. Each state has a different take on these laws, although many repeat the same provisions. The order of the chapters is determined by the population of the state, with the most populous examined first, for it is the population of the state that determines the impact of that state in the U.S. House of Representatives and in the Electoral College that selects the president. The two largest of these states, Texas and Florida, have some of the most repressive laws.

"Thanks to the extremists who now rule it, the Lone Star State is becoming a dystopia: Abortion is effectively outlawed; transgender youth and those who love them are running scared; 'CRT' panic is turning education into a vehicle for white heroism propaganda; and vigilantes have been empowered to police their neighbors.."

—Yvonne Abraham
"Extremists rule Texas.
Here's why that matters in Massachusetts,"
The Boston Globe, March 19, 2022

CHAPTER 5

TEXAS

Severity of laws:

Overview of the Role of Slavery in Texas

Population, 2020 census: 29,145,505 (2nd in nation)

Percent of population not identifying as "white": 60% (2020)

State's percentage of Electoral College votes, 2020: 7.43%

The desire to protect slavery was a dominant and likely the most dominant factor that led to the creation of Texas as part of the United States.

The area that became the State of Texas in 1845 was occupied by indigenous civilizations until the early sixteenth century when Spain took over that area and huge areas to the south and to the west. In 1810, Mexico, which then included Texas (Tejas), began obtaining its independence from Spain. After independence, the area of Tejas was too vast and too far from Mexico's central government for the government to exercise much control.

After Mexican independence, many U.S. southerners migrated to Tejas with their slaves. The Mexican government, however, was increasingly hostile to slavery. A few years after its independence, Mexico announced that any slave from outside Mexico who entered Mexico would automatically be free. Many states within Mexico had abolished slavery altogether by 1830. Prior to 1830, the Mexican state that included Tejas freed anyone born to a slave. Many slaves from the American South sought freedom by escaping to Mexico.

It was evident that Mexico would soon abolish slavery altogether. The slave-owning occupants of Tejas knew that to keep their slaves upon whom the owners relied for their livelihood, they either had to leave Tejas or become independent of Mexico. In 1836, they declared their independence and established the independent Republic of Texas.

The constitution of the new Republic provided for slavery and effectively declared that all "Blacks" were slaves unless declared to be free by the consent of Congress. This provision for slavery was what distinguished it from Mexico, which abolished slavery altogether in 1837. By becoming independent of Mexico, Texas preserved slavery until the Thirteenth Amendment banned it in 1865. Texas joined the Confederacy on March 2, 1861.

The legacy of slavery in Texas is still evident today. The University of Texas did not allow the admission of "Black" undergraduate students until 1956, ninety-one years after slavery was banned by the Thirteenth Amendment and two years after the decision in *Brown* v. *Board of Education*. Today "Blacks" account for only 5.2% of that university's enrollment in a state with a "Black" population of 12 percent.

In keeping with its racist history, Texas today still honors its slavery-infused past. Every March 2nd it honors its independence from what predictably became anti-slavery Mexico. Texas continues to honor the Confederacy with a Confederates Heroes Day holiday on January 19, the birthday of Confederate leader Robert E. Lee. In addition, it celebrates Confederate history month every April. Many monuments honoring the Confederacy and various people who fought to preserve it are scattered throughout the state. An elaborate example of this currently sits on the grounds of the State House in Austin.

These holidays and monuments keep the Confederacy alive in Texas. Celebrating the Confederacy is to celebrate a cruel time of slavery and a time when women had no right to vote and little ability to protect themselves from abuse.

This is the kind of background that is suitable for passing a law to preserve the idea of white male supremacy.

Laws
(In effect as of December 1, 2021)

The portions of the laws cited here are from the Texas Education Code, Title 2 (Public Education), Subtitle F. (Curriculum, Programs, and Services), Chapter 28 (Courses of Study; Advancement), Subchapter A (Essential Knowledge and Skills; Curriculum).

Patriotism Required

Section 28.002 (Chapter 28) of the Texas Education Code states:

> (h) The State Board of Education and each school district shall require the teaching of informed American patriotism, Texas history, and the free enterprise system in the adoption of instructional materials for kindergarten through grade 12, including the founding documents of the United

> States. A primary purpose of the public school curriculum is to prepare thoughtful, informed citizens who understand the importance of patriotism and can function productively in a free enterprise society with appreciation for the fundamental democratic principles of our state and national heritage.

"Patriotism" is what I call a "wiggle word": its meaning wiggles depending on the political views of those who talk about it. But what is remarkable about this Texas provision is that it identifies patriotism and "democratic principles" with "a free enterprise society." This identification is a political manipulation. Nowhere in the United States Constitution is "a free enterprise society" mentioned.

Thus this provision allows those enforcing the law to discipline teachers if they present a point of view that the enforcers regard as contrary to "a free enterprise society." Any governmental regulation of business could be claimed to place a restriction on free enterprise. In effect, the provision supports a very conservative political point of view, a view that sees governmental regulation as a potential enemy of freedom. Any teacher who suggests that government through regulation can improve the economic well-being of society as a whole could be disciplined under this provision for being unpatriotic and an opponent of what the law calls "the fundamental democratic principles of our state and national heritage."

Since this provision requiring the teaching of patriotism is a part of the same law that restricts discussion of racism and sexism, it is particularly repressive. The structure of the law allows an accuser or enforcer to claim that teachers who discuss racism or sexism are also subject to penalties or termination for being unpatriotic, for they are not adhering to "a primary purpose of the public school curriculum."

The 1619 Project Barred

Section 28.0022 of the Texas Education Code states:

> (W) For any course or subject, including an innovative course, for a grade level from kindergarten through grade 12:
> . . .
> (4) a teacher, administrator, or other employee of a state agency, school district, or open-enrollment charter school may not:
> . . .
> require an understanding of The 1619 Project.

The very mention of *The 1619 Project* in the context of these laws is not only an attack on the Project itself but also an attack on the *ideas* expressed in the Project. Any teacher who mentions the Project or states ideas contained within it can be accused of requiring "an understanding" of it. Since this prohibition appears in a subsection of the section requiring the teaching of patriotism, any mention in the classroom of *The 1619 Project or any of the ideas contained within it* could be considered to be unpatriotic.

In addition, a provision in subsection(a)(4)(A)(vii) of section 28.0022 bars discussion of the idea that "the advent of slavery in the territory that is now the United States constituted the true founding of the United States" — an idea associated with *The 1619 Project*.

As explained in Chapter 4, *The 1619 Project* presents documented history of U.S. racism and its adverse impact on today. This provision of the law barring *The 1619 Project* is designed to keep students ignorant of the many ideas expressed there. Without such ideas, what remains is the endorsed history that puts "white" males at the center of building the nation with at most only minor or excusable defects.

Controversy Thwarted

Section 28.0022 of the Texas Education Code states:

> (W) For any course or subject, including an innovative course, for a grade level from kindergarten through grade 12:
> (1) a teacher may not be compelled to discuss a widely debated and currently controversial issue of public policy or social affairs;
> (2) a teacher who chooses to discuss a topic described by Subdivision (1) shall explore that topic objectively and in a manner free from political bias.

What is objective and "free from political bias" depends on the perspective of the person judging. As a practical matter, this law empowers the political biases of those who enforce the law. To avoid the threat of discipline or loss of employment, a teacher whose views differ from those who are enforcing the law would be wise to avoid any discussion of anything controversial.

Another provision of the same law, Section 28.0022 describes a concept that must not be included in the classroom:

> (W) For any course or subject, including an innovative course, for a grade level from kindergarten through grade 12:
> . . .

(4) a teacher, administrator, or other employee of a state agency, school district, or open-enrollment charter school may not:

(A) require or make part of a course inculcation in the concept that:

. . .

(viii) with respect to their relationship to American values, slavery and racism are anything other than deviations from, betrayals of, or failures to live up to the authentic founding principles of the United States, which include liberty and equality.

Because this prohibition uses the rubber band word "inculcation" — which I discussed in Chapter 4 — it effectively bars reasonable discussion of a contrary concept: that slavery was an accepted value incorporated into the U.S. Constitution until the Constitution was amended following the Civil War.

Discussion of Unconscious Racism or Sexism Prohibited

Section 28.0022 of the Texas Education Code states:

(W) For any course or subject, including an innovative course, for a grade level from kindergarten through grade 12:

. . .

(4) a teacher, administrator, or other employee of a state agency, school district, or open-enrollment charter school may not:

(A) require or make part of a course inculcation in the concept that:

...

> (ii) an individual, by virtue of the individual's race or sex, is inherently racist, sexist, or oppressive, whether consciously or unconsciously

Again, the rubber band word "inculcation" effectively prohibits reasonable discussion of unconscious racism and sexism. The prohibition of the idea that someone is "inherently racist," as discussed in Chapter 4, could allow for a broader prohibition against any discussion of whether the society is inherently racist. Any mention of unconscious racism or sexism can alert a potential accuser to think there might be a violation. But that is not the law's only ambiguity. The word "oppressive" is a rubber band word that can be stretched by an accuser or enforcer, leaving the teacher in doubt of exactly what it means.

Prohibit Discussing Whether Testing for "Merit" Has A Racially Discriminatory Impact

Section 28.0022 of the Texas Code states:

> (W) For any course or subject, including an innovative course, for a grade level from kindergarten through grade 12:
> ...
> (4) a teacher, administrator, or other employee of a state agency, school district, or open-enrollment charter school may not:

(A) require or make part of a course inculcation in the concept that:

. . .

(vi) meritocracy or traits such as a hard work ethic ae racist or sexist or were created by the members of a particular race to oppress members of another race

I discussed the ideas of "merit" and "meritocracy" in Chapter 4.

Discipline

Section 28.0022 of the Texas Education Code states:

(W) . . . A school district or open-enrollment charter school may take appropriate action involving the employment of any teacher, administrator, or other employee based on the individual's compliance with state and federal laws and district policies.

This means that a teacher can be fired if the enforcers of the law think the teacher has violated it.

Cultural Vigilantism

In October 2021, Texas State Representative Matt Krause drew up lists of 850 books that should be reviewed for inappropriateness in public and school libraries. Most of the books deal with racism, sexism, abortion, and sexual preferences. He said that he is targeting materials that "might make students feel discomfort, guilt, anguish, or any other form of psychological distress because of their race or sex." Such a vague criterion means that he can list any book that discusses anything that he does not want discussed.

His list encouraged vigilantes from all over the state to ban over 800 books from Texas public school libraries. While the laws discussed here do not require the banning of books containing the subjects targeted by the laws, the laws also do not prohibit or discourage this extended interpretation. Vigilantes like Mr. Krause can use these laws as justification for their actions even though the laws themselves do not authorize them.

The Law as a Whole

These specific provisions of law are all placed under the section that requires patriotism. Thus, any teacher who is accused of violating any of these provisions is also implicitly being accused of being unpatriotic and teaching in opposition to "the fundamental democratic principles of our state and national heritage." This effectively shuts down any attempt to discuss America's history of slavery, racism or sexism in the classroom. Without such discussion, the status quo of racist and sexist oppression is preserved and only a rosy view of American history is permitted.

"If a woman in Texas has an abortion she is breaking the law, even if her pregnancy is the result of a rape. The same woman may, however, buy an AR-15 rifle capable of firing 45 rounds a minute, and she may carry a pistol on her hip when picking her toddler up from pre-school."
    — *The Economist*, "The new exceptionalism," July 9, 2022

CHAPTER 6

FLORIDA

Severity of laws:

Overview of the Role of Slavery in Florida

> Population, 2020 census: 21,538,187 (3rd in nation)
>
> Percent of population not identifying as "white": 48% (2020)
>
> State's percentage of Electoral College votes, 2020: 5.40%

To eliminate a place where runaway slaves could be safe and to remove a home of the Seminoles, Florida was forcefully taken from Spain to become a part of the United States in 1819. General Andrew Jackson, who later became President of the United States, led the invasion of the Spanish land. The former slaves and the Seminoles, who often lived together, fought together to defend their lands and their freedom but eventually were defeated. Defeated and part of the United States, the former slaves were re-enslaved and the Seminoles expelled.

In January of 1861, Florida seceded and joined the Confederacy that formed the following month, seeking again to preserve slavery.

The lasting effect of slavery and Jim Crow of the mind in Florida is indicated by the "racial" composition of the University of Florida, where only 6% of the students are "Black" in a state where 14 – 17% of the population is "Black." Due to Florida state law, the University of Florida did not allow the admission of a "Black" student until 1958, four years after the decision in *Brown* v. *Board of Education*. The Florida Supreme Court backed the delay.

Laws
(In effect as of July 1, 2022)

The portions of the law cited here are from the 2022 Florida Statutes, Title XLVIII, Chapter 1000, Section 1000.05(4). The statutes were changed by what Governor DeSantis publicly called the "Stop W.O.K.E. Act," sometimes known as House Bill No. 7. (The provocative acronym stands for "Wrongs to Our Kids and Employees.")

The severity of this law is due to one word: *advances*. It is hidden in the middle of a series of less expansive words—a rhetorical trick of politically inspired legislatures (as I discussed in Chapter 4). The law, subsection 1000.05(a), begins "It shall constitute discrimination on the basis of race, color, national origin, or sex under this section to subject any student or employee to training or instruction that espouses, promotes, *advances*, inculcates, or compels such student or employee to believe any of the following concepts" (*my emphasis added*).

The word "advances" is the broadest of these rubber-band prohibitions. To violate the law, a teacher need not espouse, promote, inculcate, or compel students to accept an idea. Merely *advancing* the idea is enough. Mention of any of the prohibited concepts is enough to accuse a teacher of advancing the concept, putting the teacher on the defensive.

The laws examined here pertain only to public primary and secondary schools. Other laws include training programs for employees and the content of classes in state-funded colleges and universities. Enforcement of both of the latter have been halted by injunctions, the fate of which depends on judicial appeals. The laws pertaining to public schools remain in place (as of the date of publication of this book).

Discussion of Unconscious Racism or Sexism Prohibited

The prohibited concepts include §1000.05 (4)(a)2: "A person, by virtue of his or her race, color, national origin, or sex, is inherently racist, sexist, or oppressive, whether consciously or unconsciously." A teacher who mentions this idea can be accused of advancing it.

Although a careful reading of the law would prevent it from being stretched to prohibit a teacher from discussing racism and sexism that are inherently present in the society though not necessarily in any particular individual, such a distinction might escape the comprehension of an accuser or enforcer. If so, the teacher would be in trouble. A teacher anticipating this problem of interpretation would not discuss it at all to be safe. Any mention of unconscious racism or sexism can alert a potential accuser to think there might be a violation.

In addition, the word "oppressive" is a rubber band word that can be stretched by an accuser or enforcer, leaving the teacher in doubt about exactly what it means.

Discussion of Societal Racism and Sexism Barred

The prohibited concepts include §1000.05(4)(a)(3): "A person's moral character or status as either privileged or oppressed is necessarily determined by his or her race, color, national origin, or sex."

Again we have narrow and broad terms connected by "or." Here it is "moral character or status." Grammatically "moral" applies to both "character" and "status." But one does not ordinarily talk about a "moral status," so a question is raised whether "status" was intended to stand alone without the modifier. "Status" would ordinarily refer to a social status, not a moral status. In America, a person's social status is significantly affected and even determined by his or her race, color, national origin, or sex. But this truth could be interpreted as a prohibited concept in Florida's law. This lack of clarity in the law gives leeway for a broad interpretation by an accuser or enforcer. A cautious teacher would be silent about this matter to avoid being accused of advancing a prohibited concept.

Affirmative Action Denied

The prohibited concepts include §1000.05(4)(a)(8): "A person, by virtue of his or her race, color, national origin, or sex, should be discriminated against or receive adverse treatment to achieve diversity, equity, or inclusion." A program of affirmative action for "Blacks" can be construed as discrimination against those who are not "Black." Effectively this prohibition bars a public school teacher from advancing anything in favor of an affirmative action program. (This provision is much broader than a similar provision in Utah's law discussed in Chapter 4.)

Criticism of Colorblindness as Racist is Prohibited

The eighth prohibited concept, §1000.05(4)(a)(8), states: "Such virtues as merit, excellence, hard work, fairness, neutrality, objectivity, and racial colorblindness are racist or sexist, or were created by members of a particular race, color, national origin, or sex to oppress members of another race, color, national origin, or sex."

That's a mouthful of words connected by "or's." Reduced to its prohibition of criticism of colorblindness, it prohibits advancing the idea that "such virtues as . . . racial colorblindness are racist. . . ."

But it is not unreasonable for a person to argue that promoting racial colorblindness is to ignore the effects of racism and, because of this, colorblindness contributes to perpetuating racism instead of combatting it. I have stated a similar view in Chapter 1. But anyone who discussed this idea as a public school teacher in Florida could be accused of advancing a prohibited concept.

Prohibit Discussing Whether Testing for "Merit" Has A Racially Discriminatory Impact

This eighth concept also prohibits discussion of the idea that "merit" can have a racist or sexist impact. I discussed the ideas of "merit" and "meritocracy" in Chapter 4.

Vacuous Exceptions

Section 1000.05(4)(b) allows for an exception to these prohibitions which "may not be construed to prohibit discussion of the concepts listed therein as part of a larger course of training or instruction, provided such training or instruction is given in an objective manner without endorsement of the concepts."

What is "objective" will be determined by the biases of those who enforce these laws. (See Chapter 4.) To discuss racism and sexism presumes that racism and sexism exist. If those who enforce these laws question the existence of these social ills, then to discuss them as though they exist is not to be "objective."

Discipline

Violation of these laws "shall constitute discrimination on the bases of race, color, national origin, or sex." Treatment of such discrimination is addressed under another law, the Florida Civil Rights Act, Title XLIV. Chapter 760, Part I. Under this law, a public school teacher who advances a prohibited concept can be subject to civil penalties including punitive damages and payment of the attorney's fees of a prevailing accuser.

The 1619 Project Barred

Although the statutes do not explicitly say this, the Florida Department of Education has adopted rule 6A-1.094124, available on its website, which contains the following:

Examples of theories that distort historical events and are inconsistent with State Board approved standards include . . . the teaching of Critical Race Theory, meaning the theory that racism is not merely the product of prejudice, but that racism is embedded in American society and its legal systems in order to uphold the supremacy of white persons. Instruction may not utilize material from The 1619 Project and may not define American history as something other than the creation of a new nation based largely on universal principles stated in the Declaration of Independence.

Cultural Vigilantism

Going beyond what the law requires, Florida school districts have banned more than 500 books ostensibly related to race, gender and gender identity issues. Governor DeSantis publicly advertises the law's prohibited concepts as the "Stop W.O.K.E. Act ," terminology intended to arouse popular passions.

In addition, twenty-eight presidents of Florida public colleges issued a letter signed on January 18, 2023, asserting that the teaching of "critical race theory" will not be supported. The law does not define "critical race theory," leaving these college presidents free to prohibit whatever they like that pertains to a study of racism in America.

The Law as a Whole

A teacher who mentions any of the prohibited concepts in the classroom can be accused of "advancing" the concept. The laws require that only the state's official version of history is acceptable in the classroom. The overall effect of these laws combined with the cited rule from the Florida Department of Education is to silence any public school teacher who wishes to expose a class or a student to an opinion that differs from the official version.

"Trump has catalyzed racism and racial resentment, misogyny, white status decline, identity threat, economic anxiety, hatred of liberal elites and rage at globalization. Now this incendiary mix is at hand for any willing politician to capitalize on. There is no shortage of takers."
—Thomas B. Edsall
"Trump Has Big Plans for 2025, and He Doesn't Care Whether You Think He'll Win,"
New York Times, Aug. 3, 2022.

CHAPTER 7

GEORGIA

Severity of laws:

Overview of the Role of Slavery in Georgia

"One of the largest sales of enslaved persons in U.S. history took place on March 2-3, 1859, at the Ten Broeck Race Course ¼ mile southwest of here." These words introduce a brief history written on a small plaque in an impoverished section of Savannah, Georgia.

The seller of these slaves was Pierce M. Butler, an insolvent grandson of Major Pierce Butler who was an original signer of the U.S. Constitution. The slaves were inherited from Major Butler. The grandson had been married to Fanny Kemble, a British actress and an abolitionist. They were divorced ten years before the sale after she became aware of the slaveholdings.

In contrast, a 48 foot towering monument to soldiers who died in the Civil War sits in a prominent Savannah park. The monument was originally called the "Confederate

> Population, 2020 census: 10,711,908 (8th in nation)
>
> Percent of population not identifying as "white": 50% (2020)
>
> State's percentage of Electoral College votes, 2020: 2.97%

Monument" and was originally intended to commemorate only the Confederate soldiers who died. The statue of a confederate soldier stands at the top of the memorial. The memorial cannot be removed, because Georgia state law prevents the removal of monuments honoring the Confederacy and its cruelest of practices. Georgia joined the Confederacy in February, 1861.

The lasting effect of slavery and Jim Crow of the mind in Georgia is indicated by the "racial" composition of the University of Georgia, where only 8.2 % of the students are "Black" in a state where 32 – 33% of the population is "Black." The University of Georgia did not allow the admission of a "Black" student until 1961, seven years after the decision in *Brown* v. *Board of Education*.

Laws
(In effect as of July 1, 2022)

In April, 2022, Georgia's governor signed into law HB 1084. In Section 1-2, it sets forth "divisive concepts" that are barred from public school education. The divisive concepts apply to "race" and racism, and not to gender and sexism. It also addresses only conscious racism. Unconscious racism is not included in the divisive concepts, indicating that maybe discussion of unconscious racism is not considered divisive. Some other wording of divisive concepts has been modified to be somewhat less repressive than similar wording in other states. Nonetheless, it will stifle discussion of racism.

Probing Racism in the U.S. is Severely Constricted

Included as a divisive concept is the view that "the United States of America is fundamentally racist." But perhaps it is. Discussing this matter is prohibited. In addition, what does "fundamentally" mean? It is a rubber band word that an accuser or enforcer can stretch to cover any probing discussion of racism in the U.S. The rubbery law functions as a draconian prohibition against discussing the extent of racism in the country.

Also included as a divisive concept is the idea that "an individual, by virtue of his or her race, is inherently or consciously racist or oppressive toward individuals of other races." As discussed in Chapter 4, a careful reading of the law would prevent it from being stretched to prohibit a teacher from discussing racism and sexism that are inherently present in the society though not necessarily in any particular individual. But a zealous accuser or enforcer may overlook such a distinction. When the teacher's guidance is not clear, the teacher may decide that it is best to remain silent.

"History in general does not, unfortunately, provide much basis for the notion that passionately held fallacies are destined to collapse simply because they are in conflict with empirical reality."
— George M. Fredrickson, *The Arrogance of Race*

CHAPTER 8

VIRGINIA

Severity of laws:

Overview of the Role of Slavery in Virginia

Virginia is the original home of American slavery, where the arrival of African slaves and their sale first occurred in 1619. It is also the home of four of the first five presidents of the United States, all four of whom were slaveholders. Virginia joined the Confederacy in April, 1861.

The lasting effect of slavery and Jim Crow of the mind in Virginia is indicated by the "racial" composition of the University of Virginia, where only 7% of the students are "Black" in a state where 22% of the population is "Black." The University admitted its first "white" male students in 1819, but did not allow the admission of "Black" undergraduates until 1955.

Population, 2020 census: 8,631,393 (12th in nation)

Percent of population not identifying as "white": 41% (2020)

State's percentage of Electoral College votes, 2020: 2.42%

Law

(In effect as of January 15, 2022)

Virginia's law consists of Executive Order Number One, signed by Governor Glenn Youngkin on January 15, 2022, who made this Order his priority right after he took office.

Unrestricted Restrictions

The most despotic feature of this Executive Order is that it contains no outer limits. The Order prohibits "advancing" "inherently divisive concepts" and lists most of the same concepts that Texas, Florida, and many other states use. But the Order states that these concepts are "any ideas" "including but not limited to" these concepts. Whereas a properly written law prescribes outer limits on the reach of the law, the Order contains no such limits. It is a law without boundaries.

The unrestricted breadth of this Order is indicated in the Order's first sentence, which announces that the Order is designed "to end the use of inherently divisive concepts, including Critical Race Theory. . . ." Since there is no definition of critical race theory in the law, it means whatever politicians and pundits say it means.

The Order even broadens "Critical Race Theory" to include "its progeny." It also accuses critical race theory (whatever that means in this context) of instructing "students to only view life through the lens of race." That description is a distorted exaggeration designed to arouse hostile emotions.

The Order also erroneously invokes federal law as somehow underpinning the Order. It states, "For the purposes of this Executive order 'inherently divisive concepts' means advancing any ideas in violation of Title IV and Title VI of the Civil Rights Act of 1964. . . ." But this federal law does not prohibit advancing concepts. It prohibits carefully defined *actions,* not ideas. This attempt to invoke federal law in connection with this Executive Order confuses what should be protected expression of a concept with action based on a concept.

The only virtue of this unbridled law is that it is an Executive Order which can be immediately rescinded by a subsequent Governor. But that could take several years and may never happen.

Cultural Vigilantism

The Governor encouraged vigilantism when he advertised a tip line to encourage parents to report anyone thought to be teaching "divisive" concepts. The tip line encourages harassment of any teacher whom a parent does not like.

"Some boards are sacking teachers over CRT. The school board in Sullivan County, Tennessee, fired Matthew Hawn for assigning an essay by Ta-Nehisi Coates, a writer on race relations, and showing pupils a performance about the idea of white privilege. Boards are also banning books: McMinn County in Tennessee removed 'Maus', a graphic novel about the Holocaust, from its middle-school curriculum."

— *The Economist*, "Once mundane, school board meeting have become battlegrounds," February 19, 2022

CHAPTER 9

TENNESSEE

Severity of laws:

Overview of the Impact of Slavery in Tennessee

Population, 2020 census: 6,910,840 (16th in nation)

Percent of population not identifying as "white": 29% (2020)

State's percentage of Electoral College votes, 2020: 2.04%

The University of Tennessee opened for "white" male students in 1794 but did not allow the admission of an undergraduate "Black" student until 1961, seven years after the Supreme Court's decision in *Brown v. Board of Education* and ninety-six years after slavery was abolished by the Thirteenth Amendment.

The delay was in keeping with the state's long history as among the leaders of racism in America. The Ku Klux Klan, which from its beginning advocated violence to preserve white supremacy, was founded in Pulaski, Tennessee, on December 24, 1865, eighteen days after the ratification of the Thirteenth Amendment.

Tennessee joined the Confederacy on June 8, 1861. As of July, 2020, Tennessee contained over 100 statues and monuments commemorating the Confederacy.

The impact of this racist history continues. In the 2019-20 school year, 24 percent of the primary and secondary students were "Black" but under 12 percent of the teachers. Ten percent of the students were Hispanic but only one percent of the teachers. At the largest campus of the University of Tennessee (in Knoxville), approximately 7% of the enrolled students are "Black" when 17% of Tennessee's population is "Black."

In this state, Jim Crow of the mind remains quite present, and its new laws are designed to keep it that way.

Laws
(In effect as of May 25, 2021)

The severity of Tennessee's laws are due to one word: *include*. Tennessee Code Section 49-6-1019 is headed "Concepts prohibited from *inclusion* or promotion in course of instruction – Withholding of state funds upon violation" (*my emphasis added*). The text begins, "(a) An LEA [local education agency; i.e. public school] or public charter school shall not *include* or promote the following concepts . . ." (*my emphasis added*).

The catch-all term "include" in this law prohibits any discussion or mention of the prohibited concepts in public school or charter school classrooms. A teacher, textbook or other course material need not *promote* any of these concepts to violate the law. Mere mention of any of them is to *include* it.

While the law states exceptions as discussed below, the exceptions are vacuous.

Discussion of Racism and Sexism Barred

The fourteen barred concepts begin with "(1) One (1) race or sex is inherently superior to another race or sex." Since this concept cannot be *included* in the classroom, it cannot be discussed. Discussion of racism and sexism, therefore, violates this law.

For the same reason, none of the following thirteen concepts can be discussed:

> (2) An individual, by virtue of the individual's race or sex, is inherently privileged, racist, sexist, or oppressive, whether consciously or subconsciously;

> (3) An individual should be discriminated against or receive adverse treatment because of the individual's race or sex;

> (4) An individual's moral character is determined by the individual's race or sex;

> (5) An individual, by virtue of the individual's race or sex, bears responsibility for actions committed in the past by other members of the same race or sex;

> (6) An individual should feel discomfort, guilt, anguish, or another form of psychological distress solely because of the individual's race or sex;

> (7) A meritocracy is inherently racist or sexist, or designed by a particular race or sex to oppress members of another race or sex;

(8) This state or the United States is fundamentally or irredeemably racist or sexist;

(9) Promoting or advocating the violent overthrow of the United States government;

(10) Promoting division between, or resentment of, a race, sex, religion, creed, nonviolent political affiliation, social class, or class of people;

(11) Ascribing character traits, values, moral or ethical codes, privileges, or beliefs to a race or sex, or to an individual because of the individual's race or sex;

(12) The rule of law does not exist, but instead is a series of power relationships and struggles among racial or other groups;

(13) All Americans are not created equal and are not endowed by their Creator with certain unalienable rights, including, life, liberty, and the pursuit of happiness; or

(14) Governments should deny to any person within the government's jurisdiction the equal protection of the law.

Vacuous Exceptions

The same statute makes four exceptions to these fourteen prohibitions. They prescribe what is allowed:

(1} The history of an ethnic group, as described in textbooks and instructional materials adopted in accordance with part 22 of this chapter;

(2) The impartial discussion of controversial aspects of history;

(3) The impartial instruction on the historical oppression of a particular group of people based on race, ethnicity, class, nationality, religion, or geographic region; or

(4) Historical documents relevant to subdivisions (b)(1) – (3) that are permitted under § 49-6-1011.

What is "impartial," like what is "objective," will be determined by the biases of accusers and those who enforce these laws. To discuss racism and sexism presumes that racism and sexism exist. If those who enforce these laws question the existence of these social ills, then to discuss them as though they exist is not to be "impartial." Teachers who want to keep their jobs would thoughtfully conclude that these topics should not be discussed at all.

Thus, the exceptions allow into the classroom only what is approved by those in charge.

The Consequences of Violation

The statute also provides for severe consequences for violation of these laws, all controlled by one person, "the commissioner":

> If the commissioner of education finds that an LEA or public charter school knowingly violated this section, then the commissioner shall withhold state funds, in an amount determined by the commissioner, from the LEA or public charter school until the LEA or public charter school provides evidence to the commissioner that the LEA or public charter school is no longer in violation of this section.

Cultural Vigilantism

The Tennessee Department of Education has an online "Prohibited Concepts Complaint Form" that any student parent of a student, or public school employee can fill out to complain about a teacher, text book or other course material.

The Law as a Whole

The Tennessee law and implementation by the state's Department of Education subjects every public school teacher to scrutiny by the public, particularly by the most reactionary members of the public who can accuse any teacher whom they do not like or any course material of presenting a "prohibited concept." The prohibited concepts are vaguely defined, giving full leeway for an accusatory interpretation. There is no room here for freedom of speech or probing discussion of the worst of the nation's ills.

Even discussion of the law itself is a prohibited concept, for to discuss it is to discuss the prohibited concepts that the law does not allow to be discussed. Students cannot even learn about the law that is stifling their education.

"Therefore it is merely the part of wisdom to try our plan, which is to try for the gradual re-enfranchisement of the worthy colored man of the South by frankly giving the leadership of our movement to the wisest and justest white men of the South."

—Theodore Roosevelt
"The Progressives and the Colored Man,"
Outlook, Aug. 24, 1912

CHAPTER 10

SOUTH CAROLINA

Severity of laws:

Overview of the Role of Slavery in South Carolina

Charleston, South Carolina has been called the slave capital of America. It is where the largest number of slaves arrived and were sold. South Carolina took the lead in creating the Confederacy. It was the first state to secede, on December 20, 1860.

The lasting effect of slavery and Jim Crow of the mind in South Carolina is indicated by the "racial" composition of the University of South Carolina, where only 10% of the students are "Black" in a state where 26% of the population is "Black." The University of South Carolina did not allow the admission of a "Black" student until 1963, nine years after the decision in *Brown* v. *Board of Education*.

Population, 2020 census: 5,118,425 (23rd in nation)

Percent of population not identifying as "white": 38% (2020)

State's percentage of Electoral College votes, 2020: 1.67%

Laws
(In effect as of July 1, 2021)

South Carolina's law restricting what teachers say in the classroom is contained in its annual budget laws for fiscal years 2021-2022 and 2022-2023 (ending June 30, 2023, unless the provision is repeated in a subsequent budget). The General Appropriations Bill for Fiscal Year 2022-2023, H.5150, Section 1.93, states (my emphasis added):

> . . . of the funds allocated by the Department of Education to school districts, no monies shall be used by any school district or school to provide instruction in, to teach, instruct, or train any administrator, teacher, staff member, or employee to adopt or believe, or to approve for use, make use of, or carry out standards, curricula, lesson plans, textbooks, instructional materials, or instructional practices that serve to *inculcate* any of the following [eight] concepts. . . .

The same paragraph was contained in the previous budget, the General Appropriations Bill for Fiscal Year 2021-2022, H.4103, Section 1.105. The listed eight prohibited concepts are similar to the prohibited concepts in effect in many of the fifteen states and cover sexism as well as racism.

Since the meaning of "inculcate" is stretchable (see Chapter 4), this paragraph on funding can reasonably be construed to mean that the salary of any teacher who provides instruction involving any of these eight concepts can be defunded either directly or indirectly by reducing funding for the school or school district.

Discussion of Unconscious Racism or Sexism in the Society May Jeopardize Funding

The second of these defundable concept states: "an individual, by virtue of his race or sex, is inherently racist, sexist, or oppressive, whether consciously or unconsciously." An accuser or enforcer may not see the difference between stating that "an individual" is inherently racist or sexist, and the society or certain social institutions are inherently racist or sexist and affect every individual. Any mention of unconscious racism or sexism can alert a potential accuser to think there might be a violation.

Discussion of Effects of Racism or Sexism on One's Standing or Worth in Society May Jeopardize Funding

The fourth defundable concept states: "an individual's moral standing or worth is necessarily determined by his race or sex." If racism and sexism are prevalent in the society, they certainly affect the societal worth and standing of individuals based on race or sex. They affect their jobs, where they live, and who they associate with. To make this a concept that cannot be funded is to prohibit discussion of the well-founded idea that racism and sexism are indeed ingrained in the society.

Discussion of Racism or Sexism that Arouses Discomfort May Jeopardize Funding

The sixth defundable concept states: "an individual should feel discomfort, guilt, anguish, or any other form of psychological distress on account of his race or sex." Anyone who does feel psychological distress from a discussion about racism or sexism can accuse a teacher of causing it, even when the teacher does not intend to cause it. Racism and sexism cannot be discussed without some discomfort. Effectively this defundable concept allows for defunding of any teacher who discusses racism and sexism, for any in-depth discussion is likely to make someone feel uncomfortable.

No law should depend on the subjective response of listener or participant where there are no standards. But that is what this budget provision does.

Prohibit Discussing Whether Testing for "Merit" Has A Racially Discriminatory Impact

The seventh defundable concept states: "meritocracy or traits such as a hard work ethic are racist or sexist, or were created by members of a particular race to oppress members of another race."

I discussed the ideas of "merit" and "meritocracy" in Chapter 4.

Discipline

The threat of defunding a teacher or a school or an entire school district is sufficient to impose upon teachers restrictions and prohibitions that will stifle any effort to discuss racism and sexism in the classroom in any but a superficial manner.

Cultural Vigilantism

The budget law gives vigilante ideas to individual schools and local school districts that go beyond the letter of the law. The Batesburg-Leesville Middle School, for example, removed a book on anti-racism from the school library, even though the budget law does not ban books. The Horry County School Board banned "critical race theory," undefined, from its classrooms, even though the budget law does not mention that term.

The Law as a Whole

Instead of affirmatively funding teaching about racism and sexism, South Carolina chooses to take funding away if either of these is taught. Here, it appears that ignorance is the best policy.

"Racism is, and always has been, the way America has sorted and ranked its people in a bitterly divisive, humanity-robbing system."
— Debby Irving, *Waking Up White*

CHAPTER 11

ALABAMA

Severity of laws:  ?

Jim Crow of the Mind in Alabama

On February 4, 1861, delegates from South Carolina, Mississippi, Florida, Georgia, Louisiana, and Alabama met in Montgomery, Alabama to form the Confederacy, dedicated to the preservation of slavery.

The public University of Alabama opened its doors to "white" male students in 1831. One hundred and twenty-five years later, in 1956, the University admitted its first acknowledged "Black" student, Autherine Juanita Foster. She lasted for two full days of classes, as vicious mobs bearing Confederate flags led the University to expel her. She did not return to the University until thirty-two years later and received her master's degree in 1992.

The legacy of slavery and its aftermath is evident at the University of Alabama, where 11% of its enrollment is "Black" in a state where 27% of the population is "Black."

> Population, 2020 census: 5,024,279 (24th in nation)
>
> Percent of population not identifying as "white": 37% (2020)
>
> State's percentage of Electoral College votes, 2020: 1.67%

Alabama now seeks to supplement its white male supremacist past with new laws designed to suppress the teaching of the United States' and Alabama's racist history.

Laws and Interpretations

Alabama "law" banning "critical race theory" is a matter of smoke and mirrors. It is dangerous nonetheless, for the law that exists currently, a one-sentence provision of the Alabama Administrative Code, Section 290-040-040-02, says little but has been proclaimed to say much more. It is plausible that more complete legislation will be signed into law in 2023, after the publication of this book, that will be as draconian as the worst laws of other states. Both houses of the legislature came close to agreeing on such a law in 2022. Governor Kay Ivey would most likely enthusiastically sign it.

On August 12, 2021, the Alabama State Board of Education passed a resolution that states (among other things):

> WHEREAS, concepts that impute fault, blame, a tendency to oppress others, or the need to feel guilt or anguish to persons solely because of their race or sex violate the premises of individual rights, equal opportunity, and individual merit, and therefore have no place in professional development for teachers, administrators, or other employees of the public educational system of the State of Alabama, and

> WHEREAS, for the same reasons, such concepts should not be taught to students in the public educational system of the State of Alabama:
>
> NOW, THEREFORE, BE IT RESOLVED, that the Alabama State Board of Education affirms that we will not support, or impart, any K-12 public education resources or standards intended to indoctrinate students in social or political ideologies that promote one race or sex above another; and
>
> BE IT FURTHER RESOLVED, That the Alabama State Board of Education recognizes that slavery and racism are betrayals of the founding principles of the United States, including freedom, equality, justice, and humanity, and that individuals living today should not be punished or discriminated against because of past actions committed by members of the same race or sex. . . .

The Governor claimed that this resolution banned "critical race theory" from the classrooms of Alabama. Of course, a mere resolution does no such thing. It is not a law. In addition, the resolution says nothing about "critical race theory."

A few months later, however, the resolution was used to amend the Administrative Code by adding section 290-040-040-02 (which is a law) to state:

> (2) The State Board of Education specifically prohibits each local board of education from offering K-12 instruction that indoctrinates students in social or political ideologies or theories that promote one race or sex above another. . . .

The actual words of this provision allow for varying interpretations and applications. The problem lies in how these words will be interpreted, which will be affected by their political and social context. The Governor has already stated that the resolution banned "critical race theory," so it is likely that the Governor and her supporters will interpret this unclear provision in the Code to mean that anything they call "critical race theory" will be banned.

In addition, the "whereas" clause of the resolution states, "concepts that impute . . . a tendency to oppress others . . . solely because of their race or sex . . . have no place. . . ." This prohibits in-depth discussion of unconscious racism and sexism. Certainly "whites" and males unconsciously absorb the dominant culture which often leads them to do oppressive things to "Blacks" and women.

This part of this "whereas" clause could be used to indicate that the resolution itself was intended to accomplish more than what the words of the resolution actually say. If this "whereas" clause is used for interpretating the amended Code, the Code would be interpreted to ban serious discussion of racism and sexism in the classroom. It is the unpredictably broad interpretations by accusers and high officials that are the danger. The Governor has already committed herself to an interpretation that goes well beyond the words themselves.

Teachers will have to be very cautious in this environment, for the Code provides that teachers who violate its vague provisions can not only be fired but also have their license to teach revoked.

"I was a 13-year-old schoolgirl on the summer morning when a nuclear weapon detonated above Hiroshima. Trapped beneath the debris, I listened to my classmates call for their mothers while they burned alive."
—Setsuko Thurlow, Survivor of Hiroshima
"Letters," *The Economist*, June 18, 2022

CHAPTER 12

KENTUCKY

Severity of laws:

Overview of the Role of Slavery in Kentucky

Prior to the ratification of the Thirteenth Amendment, the right to own slaves as property was embodied in the Kentucky Constitution. Nonetheless, Kentucky contained a strong anti-slavery component. During the Civil War, it had two purported governments, one that joined the Confederacy and one that did not.

Unlike other former members of the Confederacy, Kentucky allowed a co-educational college to be open to both "whites" and "Blacks." Berea College opened in 1855. One of my distant cousins, John H. Jackson, graduated from the college in 1874 and was reportedly the first "Black" student to do so. But the political descendants of the pro-slavery faction of the state claimed victory by passing a state law in 1904 that banned integrated college education. The U.S. Supreme Court, in *Berea College* v. *Kentucky* (1908) upheld

Population, 2020 census: 4,505,836 (26th in nation)

Percent of population not identifying as "white": 19% (2020)

State's percentage of Electoral College votes, 2020: 1.49%

the constitutionality of the law, indicating that racism was still deeply ingrained in the nation's highest court.

The lasting effect of slavery and Jim Crow of the mind in Kentucky is indicated by its impact on higher education. The University of Kentucky did not admit a "Black" student in its graduate school until 1949, 84 years after the end of the Civil War. The first undergraduate "Black" students were not allowed to enter until 1954, the year of the decision in *Brown v. Board of Education*. Four years earlier, Kentucky's law was amended to allow Berea College to admit "Black" students, after forty-six years of barring them.

Laws
(In effect as of July 14, 2022)

Kentucky Revised Statutes, Section 158.196 (through the 2022 Special Session, updated January 25, 2023) contains the following:

> A public school or public charter school shall provide instruction and instructional materials that are aligned with the social studies academic standards ... consistent with the following concepts: ... (f) The understanding that the institution of slavery and post-Civil War laws enforcing racial segregation and discrimination were contrary to the fundamental American promise of life, liberty, and the pursuit of happiness, as expressed in the Declaration of Independence, but that defining racial disparities solely on the legacy of this institution is destructive to the unification of our nation. ...

The website of the Kentucky Department of Education, on the page titled "Senate Bill 1 Guidance for School-based Decision Making," dated January, 2023, repeats the same provision that begins, "The understanding that . . . ."

Effectively Bars Discussion of *The 1619 Project* and the Idea Behind It

The provision that bars "defining racial disparities solely on the legacy of this institution [slavery]" indirectly bars discussion of *The 1619 Project* and the idea behind it. (See Chapter 4.) While *The 1619 Project* does not assert that today's racial disparities were "solely" due to slavery, this detail is likely to be lost or obscured by those who enforce or seek to enforce this provision.

"Slavery as practiced in the American South, it is now generally acknowledged, was probably as severe as any form of it in recorded history."
— Richard Kluger, *Simple Justice: The History of* Brown *v.* Board of Education *and Black America's Struggle for Equality*

CHAPTER 13

OKLAHOMA

Severity of laws:

Overview of the Role of Slavery in Oklahoma

Population, 2020 census: 3,959,353 (28th in nation)

Percent of population not identifying as "white": 39% (2020)

State's percentage of Electoral College votes, 2020: 1.30%

The territory of Oklahoma was occupied by several indigenous nations until the late nineteenth century. Some of these nations had been there for centuries and others, mostly in the early nineteenth century, had been forcibly relocated from southern states. The wealthier of many of these groups owned slaves of African descent. Slavery did not become illegal until after the Civil War. Nearly all of the indigenous peoples who fought in that war fought on the side of the Confederacy.

In 1889, "whites" were allowed into the territory, and many relocated there, pushing the indigenous peoples off of much of their land. By 1907, when Oklahoma became a state, "whites" constituted approximately three-quarters of the state's population.

During the early history of Oklahoma as a state, "Blacks" built a relatively thriving community in Tulsa. On May 31, 1921, "white" mobs began their destruction of that community, killing hundreds and leaving thousands homeless. It was the worst race riot against "Blacks" in United States history following the Civil War. The unpunished criminality of this horrendous event was followed by the unpunished suppression of knowledge of the event.

Jim Crow was deeply ingrained in the state. The University of Oklahoma opened its doors to "white" male students in 1892. Fifty-six years later, in 1948, the University admitted its first acknowledged "Black" student, George W. McLaren, 83 years after the end of the Civil War. Mr. McLaren was admitted to a graduate school program. Undergraduate programs were not desegregated until 1955.

Laws

(Emergency rule in effect as of May, 2021; extended by permanent rule on May 10. 2022.)

Oklahoma's law, known as HB 1775 but codified as Section 210: 10-1-23 in the Oklahoma statutes, sets forth eight prohibitions pertaining to the teaching of racism and sexism. Subsection I states a "general prohibition": "No teacher, administrator or other school employee shall require or make part of any Course offered in a Public School the following discriminatory principles . . . ." Examination of these principles follow.

Discussion of Racism and Sexism Thwarted

The prohibition against having a teacher "make part of any Course" a discriminatory principle permits a broad interpretation: Any mention or discussion of a discriminatory principle could be considered as making it a "part of" the course.

Number two of these prohibited discriminatory principles states: "An individual, by virtue of his or her race or sex, is inherently racist, sexist or oppressive, whether consciously or unconsciously." An accuser or enforcer may not see the difference between stating that "an individual" is inherently racist or sexist and stating that the society or certain social institutions are inherently racist or sexist and affect every individual consciously or unconsciously. The latter idea is certainly worthy of discussion. But Oklahoma's law could be interpreted to prohibit such discussion. Any mention of unconscious racism or sexism can alert a potential accuser to think there might be a violation.

Number five of these prohibited discriminatory principles states: "An individual's moral character is necessarily determined by his or her race." While a person's moral character is not determined by race, our society, due to its racism, often treats a person's moral character as altered by the person's "race." Whether discussion of the latter will also be barred by this provision will depend on the predilections of the accusers and enforcers.

Number seven of these prohibited discriminatory principles states: "Any individual should feel discomfort, guilt, anguish or any other form of psychological distress on account of his or her race or sex." Anyone who does feel psychological distress from a discussion about racism or sexism can accuse a teacher of causing it even when the teacher does not intend to cause it. Racism and sexism cannot be discussed without some discomfort. How this provision will be applied will depend on how much the accusers and enforcers want to avoid "discomfort."

Number eight of these prohibited discriminatory principles states: Meritocracy or traits such as a hard work ethic are racist or sexist or were created by members of a particular race to oppress members of another race." I discussed the ideas of "merit" and "meritocracy" in Chapter 4.

Door Opened for Cultural Vigilantism

Section 210: 10-1-23I of the law opens the door for parents to interpret the law. It states: "Parents and legal guardians of students enrolled in Public Schools in this state shall have the right to inspect curriculum, instructional materials, classroom assignments, and lesson plans to ensure compliance . . . no Public School shall interfere with or infringe upon the fundamental rights of parents to determine their child's education."

In addition, subsection (g) requires the discriminatory principles to be placed in student handbooks, and requires parents and legal guardians to be notified of these principles annually. Subsection (g)(1) states: "Public schools shall be required to develop a process for students, parents, teachers, school staff, and members of the public to file a complaint alleging a violation of the provisions of . . . this rule."

Thus, the severity of this law will depend on how the law is interpreted by politicians, pundits, parents, local school boards, schools, and students.

Discipline

Subsection (j) provides for the suspension or revocation of the license or certificate of any public school teacher, administrator, or librarian who has been determined not to have complied with this law.

"White supremacy and black degradation were institutionalized within the very framework of the new government [of the United States]."
— Richard Kluger, *Simple Justice: The History of* Brown *v.* Board of Education *and Black America's Struggle for Equality*

CHAPTER 14

IOWA

Severity of laws:

Overview

Iowa's history of racism and sexism is not significantly different from that of other northern states. It had abolished slavery long before the Civil War. Yet, in 2021 it enacted a very broad law to stifle discussion of racism and sexism in the classroom. The idea of white male supremacy appears to have taken over its politics. Racist incidents are still prevalent and may be increasing.

Population, 2020 census: 3,190,369 (31st in nation)

Percent of population not identifying as "white": 17% (2020)

State's percentage of Electoral College votes, 2020: 1.12%

Laws
(In effect as of June 8, 2021)

Iowa's laws are contained in Iowa Code Chapter 261, Section 261H.8 and Chapter 279, Section 279.74, both inserted (after corrections) by House File 802, approved by the Governor on June 8, 2021. Section 261H.8 applies to public institutions of higher education (community colleges and other state-funded colleges and universities). Section 279.74 applies to school districts which govern public primary and secondary schools. Section 279.74 incorporates prohibited concepts contained in Section 261H.8.

Discussion of Existing Racism and Sexism Banned

Both sections prohibit the teaching or promotion of race or sex scapegoating or stereotyping. Race or sex stereotyping "means ascribing . . . privileges [or] status . . . to a race or sex, or to an individual because of the individual's race or sex."

But racism and sexism largely consist of privileges and higher social status given to "whites" and males based on their "race" or sex. If this attribute of our society cannot be discussed, then racism and sexism cannot be meaningfully discussed.

Additional Specific Prohibitions

While any meaningful discussion of racism and sexism is already prohibited by the law's overly broad definition of race or sex "stereotyping," for good measure the law pertaining to higher education also adds "specific defined concepts" which are barred from the classroom.

The most draconian of these banned concepts (number (2)) is "that the United States of America and the state of Iowa are fundamentally or systematically racist or sexist." The mere presence of this prohibition in an Iowa statute is itself evidence of fundamental or systematic racism and sexism, for it is systematic racism and sexism that enabled the law to exist. But, under Iowa law, this must not be discussed in the classroom of a public institution of higher education.

Number three of these banned concepts states: "That an individual, solely because of the individual's race or sex, is inherently racist, sexist or oppressive, whether consciously or unconsciously." An accuser or enforcer may not see the difference between stating that "an individual" is inherently racist or sexist, and stating that the society or certain social institutions are inherently racist or sexist and affect every individual consciously or unconsciously. The latter idea is certainly worthy of discussion. But this provision by itself could be interpreted to prohibit such discussion. Any mention of unconscious racism or sexism can alert a potential accuser to think there might be a violation.

Number six of these "specific defined concepts" states: "That an individual's moral character is necessarily determined by the individual's race or sex." While a person's moral character is not determined by "race" or sex, our society, due to its racism and sexism, often treats a person's moral character as altered by the person's "race" or sex. Whether discussion of society's impact on us as individuals will also be barred by this provision will depend on the predilections of the accusers and enforcers.

Number eight of these "specific defined concepts" states: "That any individual should feel discomfort, guilt, anguish, or any other form of psychological distress on account of that individual's race or sex." Anyone who does feel psychological distress from a discussion about racism or sexism can accuse a teacher of causing it, even when the teacher does not intend to cause it. Racism and sexism cannot be discussed without some discomfort. How this provision will be applied will depend on how much the accusers and enforcers want to avoid "discomfort."

Number nine of these "specific defined concepts" states: "That meritocracy or traits such as a hard work ethic are racist or sexist, or were created by a particular race to oppress another race." I discussed the ideas of "merit" and "meritocracy" in Chapter 4.

While the law pertaining to primary and secondary public schools does not prohibit "specific defined concepts" (an oversight?), its prohibition against race or sex stereotyping, because of its unique and overly broad definition, is sufficient by itself to ban any serious discussion of racism and sexism in the primary and secondary schools as well as in publicly funded colleges and universities.

"The idea of 'race' represents one of the most dangerous myths of our time, and one of the most tragic."
— Ashley Montagu, *Man's Most Dangerous Myth: The Fallacy of Race,"* 1942.

CHAPTER 15

ARKANSAS

Severity of laws:

Overview of the Role of Slavery in Arkansas

Slavery was permitted and widespread in Arkansas until the enactment of the Thirteenth Amendment. Arkansas joined the Confederacy in May 1861.

In September, 1957, Little Rock was the scene of major resistance to integration of the city's high school. Governor Orval Faubus called in the Arkansas National Guard to prevent nine "Black" students from entering the school. Screaming "white" mobs supported the Governor's decision. President Eisenhower federalized the National Guard to enable the students to enter.

The legacy of slavery and Jim Crow of the mind remains evident today. At the main campus of the University of Arkansas, 5% of the students are "Black." In the state, more than 12 to 15% of the people are "Black." The university was founded in 1871. It did not permit admission of a "Black"

> Population, 2020 census: 3,011,524 (33rd in nation)
>
> Percent of population not identifying as "white": 41% (2020)
>
> State's percentage of Electoral College votes, 2020: 1.12%

student until 1948, seventy-seven years after its founding and eighty-three years after the Civil War.

Laws
(In effect as of January 1, 2022)

The Code of Arkansas, section 25-1-901, defines "divisive concepts." It was put in place by Senate Bill 627 (after renumbering), which became law on May 3, 2021, when the Governor neither signed it nor vetoed it, with an effective date eight months later.

On January 10, 2023, the new Governor, Sarah Huckabee Sanders, issued Executive Order 23-05, titled "Executive Order to Prohibit Indoctrination and Critical Race Theory in Schools." Whereas the Code lists nine divisive concepts pertaining to race and sex (including "race or sex stereotyping" and "scapegoating") the Executive Order contains only two of the Code's prohibitions but expands them beyond race and sex to also include "color, creed, . . . ethnicity, . . . age, marital status, familial status, disability, religion, national origin, or any other characteristic protected by federal or state law." In other respects, the Executive Order is less restrictive than the Code and does not override the Code's broader reach.

With minor exceptions, the Arkansas Code contains the very same restrictions on teachers as contained in the Iowa Code pertaining to institutions of higher education. Both have the same overly broad definition of race or sex stereotyping. The same "specific defined concepts" that I address in Iowa's Code are the same as the "divisive concepts" contained in the Arkansas Code. One such "divisive concept" changed a word to read, "The State of

Arkansas or the United States is fundamentally racist or sexist."

Thus, instead of repeating my discussion here, please refer to my treatment of the Iowa Code's provisions.

"Humans are not divided biologically into distinct continental types or racial genetic clusters."
— Executive Summary of the American Association of Physical Anthropologists' "Statement on Race and Racism" adopted March 27, 2019.

CHAPTER 16

NEW HAMPSHIRE

Severity of laws:

Overview

Slavery was legal in New Hampshire until 1857, prior to the Civil War, not unlike many other northern states during that time. The study of systematic racism and its denial in New Hampshire would take us beyond the scope of this book. Like Iowa in many respects, New Hampshire is an example of how denial that systematic racism exists is itself a product of systematic racism. Such denial has led to state law that makes examination of systematic racism not possible in the public schools. Systematic sexism is also included as something that must not be studied in the public schools. In New Hampshire, protecting ignorance of racism and sexism is now the law of the state.

> Population, 2020 census: 1,377,529 (41st in nation)
>
> Percent of population not identifying as "white": 13% (2020)
>
> State's percentage of Electoral College votes, 2020: 0.74%

Laws
(In effect as of June 25, 2021)

New Hampshire Revised Statutes, Section 193:40, contains three prohibited concepts that may not be taught in the public schools.

Stifles the Teaching of Unconscious Racism or Sexism

The second of these three prohibitions state:

> No pupil in any public school in this state shall be taught . . .
> (b) That an individual, by virtue of his or her age, sex, gender identity, sexual orientation, race, creed, color, marital status, familial status, mental or physical disability, religion, or national origin, is inherently racist, sexist, or oppressive, whether consciously or unconsciously

As in other states that have similar prohibitions, an accuser or enforcer may not see the difference between stating that "an individual" is inherently racist or sexist and stating that the society or certain social institutions are inherently racist or sexist and affect every individual consciously or unconsciously. The latter idea is certainly worthy of discussion. But this prohibition could be interpreted to prohibit such discussion. Any mention of unconscious racism or sexism can alert a potential accuser to think there might be a violation.

Discipline

Part III of the law states:

> Any person claiming to be aggrieved by a violation of this section, including the attorney general, may initiate a civil action against a school or school district in superior court for legal or equitable relief, or with the New Hampshire commission for human rights as provided in RSA 354-A:34.

Part IV of the law states: "Violation of this section by an educator shall be considered a violation of the educator code of conduct that justifies disciplinary sanction by the state board of education."

Cultural Vigilantism

The New Hampshire Department of Education has a form on its website inviting people to complain about anyone thought to have taught any of the prohibited concepts in the classroom. The website states:

> Schools are prohibited from teaching that one identified group (a group based upon: age, sex, gender identity, sexual orientation, race, creed, color, marital status, familial status, mental or physical disability, religion or national origin) is:
>
> 1. Inherently superior or inferior to people of another identified group;

2. Inherently racist, sexist, or oppressive, whether consciously or unconsciously;

3. Should be discriminated against or receive adverse treatment; or

4. Should not treat members of other identified groups equally.

Parents, students and teachers who feel that these discriminatory practices have not been followed [sic] may file a complaint here: [link].

On November 18, 2021, the *Boston Globe* reported, "After the state Department of Education set up a website last week to collect complaints against teachers, The New Hampshire chapter of Moms for Liberty tweeted 'We've got $500 for the person that first successfully catches a public school teacher breaking this law.' In a follow up, the conservative parents' organization told supporters to designate online donations as 'CRT Bounty's,' referring to critical race theory." The "Moms for Liberty" website still offers a monetary incentive to report teachers.

"The legacy of the past racism directed at blacks in the United States is more like a bacillus that we have failed to destroy, a live germ that not only continues to make some of us ill but retains the capacity to generate new strains of a disease for which we have no certain cure."
—George M. Fredrickson, *Racism: A Short History*

CHAPTER 17

MONTANA

Severity of laws:

Overview

In the territory that became Montana, there were few "Blacks" and little slavery. However, slavery was permitted for eleven years until the Thirteenth Amendment was ratified in 1865.

Population, 2020 census: 1,084,225 (44th in nation)

Percent of population not identifying as "white": 17% (2020)

State's percentage of Electoral College votes, 2020: 0.74%

The most egregious racism in Montana is directed at the indigenous peoples. Recently, the state legislature sought to restrict the right to vote in a way that would have disproportionally impacted indigenous peoples. The courts have often struck down discriminatory legislation, but the attempts to suppress the vote of the indigenous peoples continues.

The plight of the indigenous peoples in Montana is thoroughly documented in a 199-page court decision nullifying discriminatory legislation designed to suppress indigenous peoples' right to vote: *Montana Democratic Party, et. al.* v. *Jacobsen*, Montana Thirteenth Judicial District Court

Yellowstone County, Consolidated Case No.: DV 21-0451 (Sept. 30, 2022).

The recent effort to suppress "critical race theory" is likely fed by the awareness that it could expose the continuing systematic oppression of the indigenous peoples.

Law
(In effect as of May 27, 2021)

The harmful provisions of Montana law are contained in the legal opinion of Attorney General Austin Knudsen, dated May 27, 2021, written in response to an inquiry from the Superintendent of Public Instruction. It is unclear, however, when Mr. Knudsen is presenting his view of the law and when he is presenting his philosophical opinions. They blend together. As I pointed out in Chapter 3, the legal analysis is both beside the point and fatally flawed. Nonetheless, his opinion is currently the law of Montana.

Bars Discussion of "Racial" Privileges and Social Status

Under the section of Mr. Knudsen's opinion headed "E. Analysis and Conclusions of Law" (which does not begin until page 18 of his opinion), he states: "Government entities may not engage in racial stereotyping, which means *ascribing* character traits, values, moral and ethical codes, *privileges, status,* or beliefs to a race or to an individual because of his or her race." (My emphasis added.) Yet, the essence of racism in our society involves giving privileges and higher social status to "whites" based on their "race."

Under Mr. Knudsen's opinion, this point of view gets defined as prohibited "racial stereotyping."

While he gives lip service to the First Amendment and to freedom of expression, this prohibition pertains to "ascribing," which is a matter of speech.

Bars Discussion of Unconscious Bias

Under Mr. Knudsen's opinion headed "E. Analysis and Conclusions of Law" he states: "Government entities also may not engage in 'race scapegoating,' which means assigning fault, blame, or *bias* to a race or to members of a race because of their race. . . . *This encompasses any claim* that, consciously or unconsciously, and by virtue of his or her race, members of any race are inherently racist or are inherently inclined to oppress others." (My emphasis added.)

Yet, racism in our society involves both conscious and unconscious widespread bias. Under Mr. Knudsen's opinion, making any claim about this point of view is prohibited "racial scapegoating." This overly broad characterization of "race scapegoating" itself reflects a bias against discussing bias.

While he gives lip service to the First Amendment and to freedom of expression, this prohibition pertains to "any claim," which is a matter of speech.

Opens Door to Letting "Discomfort" Determine Course Content

Under Mr. Knudsen's opinion headed "E. Analysis and Conclusions of Law" he states: "a school that permits, promotes, or endorses curricula or pedagogical methods that tell an individual that he or she should feel discomfort, guilt, anguish, or any other form of psychological distress on account of his or her race, almost certainly creates a racially hostile environment."

Here Mr. Knudsen confuses a subjective feeling of "discomfort, guilt, anguish, or any other form of psychological stress" with the non-subjective standard used in law for determining the presence of a hostile environment.

The U.S. Equal Employment Opportunity Commission states that, in addition to a subjective feeling, the standard for a hostile work environment must include what a "reasonable person" would consider to be hostile. The "reasonable person" standard has a long history in American law and prevents undue reliance on subjective reactions. Mr. Knudsen's opinion ignored this standard. In addition, it is not clear how the law of hostile work environment would extend to students in a classroom. Mr. Knudsen's opinion ignored this issue too. Accordingly, his opinion concerning what constitutes a racially hostile environment in the classroom is without legal merit.

Anyone who does feel discomfort or any psychological distress from a discussion about racism or sexism can accuse a teacher of causing it even when the teacher does not intend to cause it. Racism and sexism cannot be discussed without some discomfort.

Stifles Reasonable and Beneficial Advice

Mr. Knudsen also states: "A school may not advocate that students adopt specific beliefs based on their race. . . ." Thus a teacher who says, "White people should not adopt beliefs that discriminate against Black people or Asians, and Black people and Asians should not adopt beliefs that discriminate against White people," would be violating this prohibition. The safest way to avoid Mr. Knudsen's prohibitions is to be silent.

"'Race' itself is a fiction, one that has no basis in biology or any long-standing, consistent usage in human culture."
—Jacqueline Jones, *A Dreadful Deceit*

CHAPTER 18

SOUTH DAKOTA

Severity of laws:

Overview

Prior to the Civil War there was little significant slavery in the territory that became the Dakotas. After the Civil War, the Thirteenth Amendment made it illegal everywhere in the country.

The most blatant racism in South Dakota, however, is against the indigenous peoples, even extending to recent denial of hotel accomodations in violation of the federal Civil Rights Act of 1964. Jim Crow lives there today as persistent discrimination against the indigenous peoples.

Population, 2020 census: 886,667 (46th in nation)

Percent of population not identifying as "white": 15% (2020)

State's percentage of Electoral College votes, 2020: 0.74%

As shown in *Rosebud Sioux Tribe* v. *Barnett* (2022), state agencies are implicated in the attempt to suppress the vote of indigenous peoples.

Laws
(In effect as of July 1, 2022)

South Dakota enacted a prohibition against "divisive concepts" contained in its Codified Laws Section 13-1-67.

On July 29, 2021, Governor Kristi Noem signed a curious Executive Order that refrained from limiting discussion of racism and sexism in the classroom. Whereas a "Whereas" clause contains the statement, "The work of Kendi and the 1619 Project are infused with factual errors, including the statement that 'capitalism is essentially racist,' that 'racism runs in the very DNA of this country,' that our nation is not a democracy but a 'slaveocracy,' that our nation was born not with the Declaration of Independence in 1776 . . . but rather in 1619, when slavery was first introduced to the colonies . . . ," she uses this clause to disagree with the standards of federal grant proposals and therefore orders all state Department of Education officials to "refrain from applying for any federal grants in history or civics until after the 2022 South Dakota legislative session." What she calls "factual errors" are not about facts but about legitimate points of view that should be open for discussion. Nonetheless, this Executive Order itself does not appear to pose a major problem for teachers in the classroom.

Stifles the Teaching of Unconscious Racism or Sexism

One of the "divisive concepts" contained in Section 13-1-67 is "That an individual, by virtue of their race, color, religion, sex, ethnicity, or national origin is inherently racist, sexist, or oppressive, whether consciously or subconsciously."

As in other states that have a similar prohibition, an accuser or enforcer may not see the difference between stating that "an individual" is inherently racist or sexist and stating that the society or certain social institutions are inherently racist or sexist and affect every individual consciously or unconsciously. The latter idea is certainly worthy of discussion. But this prohibition could be interpreted to prohibit such discussion. Any mention of unconscious racism or sexism can alert a potential accuser to think there might be a violation.

Opens Door to Letting "Discomfort" Determine Course Content

Another of these "divisive concepts" states: "An individual should feel discomfort, guilt, anguish, or any other form of psychological distress on account of the individual's race, color, religion, ethnicity, or national origin." Anyone who does feel psychological distress from a discussion about racism or sexism can accuse a teacher of causing it even when the teacher does not intend to cause it. Racism and sexism cannot be discussed without some discomfort. How this provision will be applied will depend on how much the accusers and enforcers want to avoid "discomfort."

Additionally May Limit Discussion of the Impact of Racism and Sexism

Another of these "divisive concepts" states: "That an individual's moral character is inherently determined by their individual's race, color, religion, sex, ethnicity, or national origin or sex." While a person's moral character is not determined by "race" or sex, our society, due to its racism and sexism, often treats a person's moral character as altered by the person's "race" or sex. Whether discussion of society's impact on us as individuals will also be barred by this provision will depend on the predilections of the accusers and enforcers.

Prohibit Discussing Whether Testing for "Merit" Has A Racially Discriminatory Impact

Another of these "divisive concepts" states: "Meritocracy or traits such as a strong work ethic are racist or sexist or were created by members of a particular race or sex to oppress members of another race or sex."

I discussed the ideas of "merit" and "meritocracy" in Chapter 4.

"The major conclusion she had reached already — that wherever you went in this fractious world, people were essentially the same and had to be treated with simple (socialist) fairness."

— "Have bike, will travel,"
The Economist (June 11, 2022),
from travel writer Dervla Murphy's obituary.

CHAPTER 19

NORTH DAKOTA

Severity of laws:

Overview

The Dakota Territory was created in 1861. As with South Dakota, there was little significant slavery and none after the enactment of the Thirteenth Amendment. In 1889, the territory became the states of North Dakota and South Dakota

The most blatant racism in North Dakota, however, is against the indigenous people. As in South Dakota, the North Dakota legislature sought to suppress the vote of the indigenous peoples. The indigenous peoples and their supporters were successful, however, in getting a favorable settlement of their lawsuit against the state, *Spirit Lake Tribe et al.*, v. *Alvin Jaeger* (settled April 24, 2020).

As in Montana and South Dakota, North Dakota's effort to suppress "critical race theory" likely reveals its fear that its systematic racism against the indigenous peoples will be more fully exposed.

Population, 2020 census: 779,094 (47th in nation)

Percent of population not identifying as "white": 18% (2020)

State's percentage of Electoral College votes, 2020: 0.56%

Laws
(In effect as of November 12, 2021)

North Dakota's barrier to discussing racism in the public schools is contained in North Dakota Century Code Section 15.1-21-05.1

Broadly Bans Discussion Whether Racism is Systematically Embedded in American Society

The law states: "A school district or public school may not include instruction relating to critical race theory in any portion of the district's required curriculum under sections 15.1-21-01 or 15.1-21-02, or any other curriculum offered by the district or school. For purposes of this section, 'critical race theory' means the theory that racism is not merely the product of learned individual bias or prejudice, but that racism is systemically embedded in American society and the American legal system . . . ."

At least North Dakota law defines "critical race theory." Nonetheless, the provision bans any in-depth discussion of racism. The inclusion of such a ban in state law is itself evidence that racism is systematically embedded in American society and law. But this cannot be discussed in public school classrooms.

"I believe that in this time, when the idea of a better America, diverse, open, tolerant, and civilized, is everywhere under assault, it falls to us, to all of us, writers, publishers, booksellers, readers, citizens, to be the guardians of the culture. To be, in what we say and how we act, embodiments and protectors of that better America. . . . So perhaps there is an army of the good, an army of peace and justice, united against hate, that will stand in the way of the forces unleashed against us."
— Salman Rushdie, *Languages of Truth: Essays 2003 – 2020*

CHAPTER 20

The Danger: What Lies Ahead?

Are these state laws a prelude to increased racism and sexism throughout the country? Are they the beginning of something much worse?

It is not just these state laws that cast a dark cloud over our expectations for the future. In 2022 the United States Supreme Court reversed *Roe* v. *Wade,* the case that had for almost fifty years provided each woman with some protection to determine for herself whether to terminate a pregnancy. The composition of the Court today leads us to wonder whether it will continue to undermine national human rights that have been established over the previous several decades. The Court cannot be relied on to stop the advance of white male supremacy in state laws.

A history of antisemitism in Europe, which grew in the late nineteenth century and led to the Holocaust decades later, provides a frightening example of how racism festers and grows. This growth over several decades is poignantly chronicled in Edmund De Waal's *The Hare with Amber Eyes: A Family's History of Art and Loss.* First there is the antisemitism of individuals. Later antisemitic individuals form organizations and associations and become a political force. The openly antisemitic Karl Lueger became mayor of Vienna in 1897, the threat of which Johannes Brahms foretold with many ominous tones in his Fourth Symphony. During World War I, the idea was put forward that Jews should be expelled from Europe. Before Hitler rose to power, Alfred Rosenberg wrote popular books proclaiming that the Germans were a pure race that should conquer other nations and expel all Jews.

These were the seeds that grew into a horrifying forest. In 1933, Adolf Hitler came to power in Germany. In 1938, Jews and their businesses were violently attacked by mobs supported by the police. A policy of Aryanization took control. Jews were expelled from their homes, their businesses and jobs. The Holocaust followed during World War II.

The Holocaust was the product of many decades of antisemitic expansion in Europe. In the latter half of the nineteenth century, many Jews had become wealthy and mostly integrated into the life of major cities. Antisemitism was quite present, but like the early stages of an infection its dangers were largely unseen or passively accepted. But the infection festered until it erupted into something that could not be stifled. The earlier but spreading idea of "race" nourished this infection and enabled this sickness to become the dominant reason for genocide.

Are these state laws new infections that will erupt in future racist devastation, or the scarred leaves falling from the dying branches of the past? Will a future president of the United States be another avowed racist like Karl Lueger?

The answer lies in what we do today. If we do not remove these state laws, they will lead to new generations of ignorant people who are more easily persuaded by the appeals of tyrants. These laws are not just about several states but about the fabric of the nation as a whole. These state laws further rip the national fabric, and either we sew it up now or it will rip even more until the nation is completely torn apart, far more so than today.

ACKNOWLEDGMENTS

Over many decades, numerous people have contributed to the experiences that made this book possible. They include friends, family, teachers, colleagues and ancestors. I could not possibly name them all, so I will not try. I thank Barbara Mende for her editing assistance. I thank my wife for her constant companionship and love. I thank my son for the enrichment that he has brought to our lives.

EPILOGUE

Searching for Reality in the Face of Myths and Lies

I am the product of slavery. The likely but unknown scenario based on known historical events is that my ancestors were the result of the sexual union of European male slave owners and African female slaves. I do not know most of the details affecting me personally, but I do know that genetic tests of my son show that his father has mostly European genes from his male lineage.

In this I am not unique and am actually quite ordinary. The truth is that nearly everyone in America who is called "Black," "African-American" or "Negro" has partial European ancestry. In many cases, the European part exceeds fifty percent. Our language falsely denies this reality. That is one of the reasons why I put these "racial" terms in quotation marks. Calling some people "white" is another lie. Many of these "white" people had the same slave-owner-and-slave ancestors as "Black" people. As we can observe today, sometimes the children of "white"-"black" couples will look "white." Many "white"-looking children subsequently lived as "white." They subsequently spread African genes throughout the "white" population.

Since I view this false "racial" terminology to be of great importance, I return to this subject that I introduced in Chapter 1 and elaborated on in Chapter 2.

I put these terms in quotation marks, because they were used to justify the oppression of people not "white": oppression through slavery, colonialism, segregation, or social stratification, with "whites" on top. These "racial" terms are terms derived from oppression. I will not allow oppressors of the past or present to define who I am. I will also not allow those who suffered from this oppression in the past or present, but who in the present have accepted the categories of the oppressors, to define who I am. This terminology of oppression is not about a biological reality but is an essential tool of social and political oppression. The history of this oppression has thoroughly embedded the madness of "racial" identity into the American psyche, so much so that it is considered normal. The best we can do now to extract ourselves from this madness is to put all "racial" terminology in quotation marks, because these terms do not describe who we really are as human beings. But they do describe how we have mistakenly categorized ourselves for centuries, categorizations that obscure our seeing ourselves as unique individuals fundamentally like all other individuals.

If you think I am mad, I have the science of genetics and anthropological studies on my side, as I explained in Chapter 2. In addition, documented histories, archeology, and genetics reveal that humans for hundreds of thousands of years migrated widely and interbred with other humans and human ancestors from different groups and locations. There is no way a pure "race" could have emerged or survived. Migrations, commerce, and wars mixed one group with another. The ignoring or rejection of the findings of science and documented history and archeology is the continuing madness of "racial" divisions.

Because of the depth of this madness, we cannot abandon these "racial" terms altogether. We have to use them to discuss their deleterious effects, effects that are thoroughly ingrained into our minds and the fabric of our society. But if we do not put these terms in quotation marks, we perpetuate this madness, destroying any hope of attaining a truly democratic society.

It is only because of the impact of this mistake that it is important today to acknowledge our mixed ancestries. My mixed ancestry is just an example. It is nothing to be ashamed of or proud of. It is simply a fact. It is also a fact that everyone is a mixture, for there is no such thing as a pure race. How the more modern mixtures came about for "Blacks" is most often the way I described it for me. But it did not always happen that way. There are records of "white" women bearing the children of their slaves. Some "Blacks" were never slaves. In addition, some intimacies between slave owners and slaves were consensual. A few slave owners and slaves ended up living together and would have married if the laws had permitted it. In some cases the slave owners were indigenous people, not Europeans. There were many variations. No one story fits all.

Some details affecting me personally I do know, though I know only a few bits and pieces of the whole story. The after-effects of slavery led to my paternal grandparents meeting, marrying, and having two children, one of them my father.

A critical piece happened when my paternal grandmother and three of her sisters, in the early twentieth century, courageously left the former slave state of Kentucky where they were barred from non-segregated higher education and went west to the former anti-slavery state of Kansas, ending up in Kansas City, Kansas. Around the same time, my paternal grandfather also went to the same city to take a job as a physics teacher at the segregated "Black" high school. He had left Indiana with a college degree from the University of Indiana, where he was not allowed to live on campus because he was "Black."

Thus, I am intimately connected to the history of slavery and anti-slavery in America. Kentucky barred "Blacks" from non-segregated higher education with a law passed in 1904 and upheld by the U.S. Supreme Court in *Berea College v. Kentucky* (211 U.S. 45, 1908). This despicable act of racism—by both the state of Kentucky and the U.S. Supreme Court—was the product of slavery. My grandparents went to Kansas, because they got opportunities there that were not available in Kentucky or Indiana or neighboring Missouri. Nonetheless, Kansas City, Kansas was a segregated city. They had to live in an all-"Black" community, another outcome of slavery. I lived in this community too, where the poor and middle-class professionals lived side by side. My grandfather became principal of the community's high school and helped thwart an attempt to convert it into a trade school. The school attracted excellent teachers and produced many who became college graduates. These included me, my father, and his sister. It was in college where my father met my mother in a chemistry class. All of them graduated from the University of Kansas with Phi Beta Kappa keys. Had my grandmother remained in Kentucky, none of this would have been possible. And she would have never met my grandfather.

So I am a product of this history. Accordingly, I seek the truth of this history and do not want it deformed or suppressed by the new state laws that would ban this book and others from the public schools and libraries.

I think about what would have happened if my grandmother had decided to stay in Kentucky. Her children would have had their aspirations chopped off by a state that denied that they could go to the state's best colleges. They would not have aspired to be what the state said they could not be. There would not have been a chemist in our family. Maybe no one would have yet uncovered the inner workings of the Maillard reaction, for it was my father who did it.

Instead, she left with her sisters to start a new life in Kansas City, Kansas, and history has changed as a result. But what of the "Black" people who remained in Kentucky? They remained under the thumb of a state that would not let them be free. Their minds were enslaved.

Can this damage be repaired? No. You cannot now give education to those who were denied it. You cannot give smiles to those who suffered as slaves. You cannot remove the tears of children who saw their parents taken away, sold to another owner. You cannot replace the necks of those who were lynched without trial.

The idea of reparations is a small inadequate one that cannot do what it wished it could do. It is a noisily puffing little engine that couldn't. And in America, the idea of limiting reparations to the descendants of former slaves is myopic. You cannot select who should get reparations and who shouldn't without perpetuating the false idea of "race."

Take a look at America, not to mention elsewhere, at the suffering America's arrogant use of power has caused and ask, How do you repair it?

How do you repair the lives of the indigenous peoples who died or were relocated by the European invaders?

How do you repair the suffering of the Chinese laborers who built the railroads?

How do you restore the lives of Japanese-Americans who were rounded up and incarcerated during World War II, their property and belongings stolen from them due to the U.S. government?

How do you replace the lives of several hundreds of thousands of Japanese civilians in World War II who were deliberately targeted for death by the American and Allied firebombings of Japanese cities punctuated by two atomic bombs dropped on heavily populated areas, the aspirations of parents and children snuffed out by horrible deaths. These were vicious, atrocious war crimes by the standards of today.

How do you repair the lives of workers who lost not only their jobs but their pensions when companies abandoned where they had been for decades to pursue greater profits for their wealthiest stockholders at the expense of the people who built the companies through their daily labor?

How do you replace the past of a country that did not guarantee women the right to vote until 1920, and that still denies them equal rights by the nation's failure to ratify the Equal Rights Amendment and by its failure today to give women the right to their own bodies?

None of this can be repaired.

We can, however, look forward to a better future if we have the will and strength to build it. In such a future, we will get much closer to the realization that life in the present needs to change for something better. The idea of "all people are created equal" is aspirational. We still do not fully know what it would mean.

In my view, it would mean that everyone works to support everyone else. It means creating governmental mechanisms that ensure that everyone, without exception, receives enough to eat (unless everyone is starving), has shelter (unless no one does), has health care (unless no one does), and is supported in their aspirations to live fulfilling lives. It is what Anu Partanen called the "well-being" society. I aspire to a well-being world, not limited to any one country or region.

When Ludwig von Beethoven incorporated the words of Schiller's poem into the final movement of his Ninth Symphony, proclaiming "alle Menschen werden brüder," he made the point musically by incorporating into that movement a simple hypnotic tune from street musicians, people regarded as lowly beggars. In this way he announced to an elite audience that "alle Menschen" included those at the bottom of society. The European Union adheres to this vision with its adoption of a musical passage from the Ninth Symphony as the European Anthem.

Meanwhile, in the United States, that vision is suffocated by people who starve, who go without health care, who are denied the right to choose what happens to their own bodies if they are pregnant, and whose minds are stifled by state laws designed to suppress what they learn and what they can say.

Can't we do better than this? If we do not repudiate the laws that suppress people and deny them their right to determine their own lives, the answer is "No." And if that is the answer, we can only hope that aspiring to the goal of full democracy will be carried forth by others, for America will have failed.

Who or what is to blame for such failure? It is not any particular person or identifiable group of people. It is not any particular system of government or institution. It is simply an idea, a concept, an ideology, a belief that one group of people is inherently superior to another.

— John L. Hodge, March, 2023

NOTES AND SOURCES, Chapter by Chapter

Because much of the text is the outcome of combining many various sources including my personal experiences, footnotes would have been unwieldly. Sources are listed below for each chapter. Online sources were accessed again and confirmed on March 20, 2023.

Preface — Notes

The quotation from *Cultural Bases of Racism and Group Oppression* is from the Preface, page *ix*.

The quotation from *Overcoming the Lie of "Race": A Personal, Philosophical and Political Perspective* (second edition) is from the Epilogue, page 137.

The quotation from *Presidential Racism: The Words of U.S. Presidents Since the Civil War* is from the Preface, page 1.

The quotation from *How We Are Our Enemy – And How to Stop* is from Chapter 5, page 129.

Preface — Sources

Barry, John M. *Roger Williams and The Creation of the American Soul: Church, State and the Birth of Liberty* (New York: Viking, 2012).

Brown, Cynthia Stokes, ed., *Alexander Meiklejohn: Teacher of Freedom* (Berkeley, CA: Meiklejohn Civil Liberties Institute, 1981).

De Waal, Edmund, *The Hare with Amber Eyes: A Hidden Inheritance* (New York: Farrar, Straus and Giroux, 2012)

Grayling, A.C., *Descartes: The Life and Times of a Genius* (New York : Walker & Co., 2006).

Hodge, John L., "Democracy and Free Speech: A Normative Theory of Society and Government," Chapter 5 of *The First Amendment Reconsidered*, ed. B. F. Chamberlin & C. J. Brown (New York and London: Longman, 1982), and sources cited therein.

Hodge, John L., "Equality: Beyond Dualism and Oppression," Chapter 6 of *Anatomy of Racism*, ed. David Theo Goldberg (Minneapolis: Univ. of Minnesota Press, 1990), and sources cited therein.

Hodge, John L, *How We Are Our Enemy – And How to Stop: Our Unfinished Task of Fulfilling the Values of Democracy* (Jamaica Plain, Mass.: John L. Hodge, Publisher, 2011), and sources cited therein.

Hodge, John L, *Overcoming the Lie of "Race": A Personal, Philosophical, and Political Perspective*, Second Edition (Jamaica Plain, Mass.: John L. Hodge, Publisher, 2017), and sources cited therein.

Hodge, John L., *Presidential Racism: The Words of U.S. Presidents Since the Civil War, and an Essay: The Enduring Anti-Democratic Disease Afflicting Us – And Its Cure* (Jamaica

Plain, Mass.: John L. Hodge, Publisher, 2020), and sources cited therein.

Hodge, John L., Donald K. Struckmann and Lynn Dorland Trost, *Cultural Bases of Racism and Group Oppression: An Examination of Traditional "Western" Concepts, Values and Institutional Structures Which Support Racism, Sexism and Elitism* (Berkeley, Calif.: Two Riders Press, 1975), and sources cited therein.

Part I and Part IV of this book are reprinted in *Race and Culture in America*, 3rd edition, ed. C. E. Jackson and E. J. Tolbert (Edina MN: Burgess International Group, 1989).

Kluger, Richard, *Simple Justice: The History of* Brown v. Board of Education *and Black America's Struggle for Equality* (New York: Vintage Books, 2004).

Lewis, Anthony, *Freedom for the Thought That We Hate: A Biography of the First Amendment* (New York: Basic Books, 2007).

Mill, John Stuart, *On Liberty* (Indianapolis: Bobbs-Merrill, 1956).

Mill, John Stuart and Harriet Taylor Mill, *Essays on Sex Equality*, ed. Alice S. Rossi (Chicago and London: University of Chicago Press, 1970).

Noonan, John T., *The Antelope: The Ordeal of the Recaptured Africans in the Administration of James Monroe and John Quincy Adams* (Berkeley, CA: The University of California Press, 1977).

Plessy v. *Ferguson*, 163 U.S. 537 (1896).

Polanyi, Michael, *The Tacit Dimension* (Garden City, N.Y.: Doubleday, 1966)

The Economist "A self-repressing society," May 14, 2022, p. 42.

The Economist, "The Communist Party: Control the present, control the past," November 6, 2021, pp. 37-38.

Turberville, A. S., *Medieval Heresy and the Inquisition* (London: Archon Books, 1964; originally published in 1920).

Yalom, Irvin D., *The Spinoza Problem: A Novel* (New York: Basic Books, 2012).

Chapter 1 — Notes

The statement, "The idea [of "race"] began to emerge in the laws of some American colonies around 350 years ago," is documented in my book, *Overcoming the Lie of "Race,"* Chapter 4, pp. 48 ff, with sources cited therein.

The content of Chapter 1 is based on many various combinations of multiple sources listed below and from personal experience.

Chapter 1 — Sources

Declaration of Independence, July 4, 1776.

Freire, Paulo, *Pedagogy of the Oppressed*, trans. M. B. Ramos (New York: Seabury Press, 1970).

Hannah-Jones, Nikole, et. Al., editors, *The 1619 Project* (New York: One World, 2021).

Hodge, John L, *How We Are Our Enemy – And How to Stop: Our Unfinished Task of Fulfilling the Values of Democracy* (Jamaica Plain, Mass.: John L. Hodge, Publisher, 2011), and sources cited therein.

Hodge, John L, *Overcoming the Lie of "Race": A Personal, Philosophical, and Political Perspective,* Second Edition (Jamaica Plain, Mass.: John L. Hodge, Publisher, 2017), and sources cited therein.

Hodge, John L., *Presidential Racism: The Words of U.S. Presidents Since the Civil War, and an Essay: The Enduring Anti-Democratic disease Afflicting Us – And Its Cure* (Jamaica Plain, Mass.: John L. Hodge, Publisher, 2020), and sources cited therein.

Hodge, John L., Donald K. Struckmann and Lynn Dorland Trost, *Cultural Bases of Racism and Group Oppression: An Examination of Traditional "Western" Concepts, Values and Institutional Structures Which Support Racism, Sexism and Elitism* (Berkeley, Calif.: Two Riders Press, 1975), and sources cited therein.

Part I and Part IV of this book are reprinted in *Race and Culture in America,* 3rd edition, ed. C. E. Jackson and E. J. Tolbert (Edina MN: Burgess International Group, 1989).

Shetterly, Margot Lee, *Hidden Figures: The American Dream and the Untold Story of the Black Women Mathematicians Who Helped Win the Space Race* (New York: William Morrow, 2016).

The Economist, "The real culture warriors," Jan. 14, 2023, p. 26.

Weinstein, Rhona S., *Reaching Higher: The Power of Expectations in Schooling* (Cambridge, Mass.: Harvard Univ. Press, 2002).

On-line Sources:

"Nikole Hannah-Jones Issues Statement on Decision to Decline Tenure Offer at University of North Carolina-Chapel Hill and to Accept Knight Chair Appointment at Howard University," July 6, 2021:
https://www.naacpldf.org/press-release/nikole-hannah-jones-issues-statement-on-decision-to-decline-tenure-offer-at-university-of-north-carolina-chapel-hill-and-to-accept-knight-chair-appointment-at-howard-university/

"The link between voting rights and the abortion ruling," *Washington Post*, June 28, 2022:
https://www.washingtonpost.com/outlook/2022/06/28/dobbs-voting-rights-minority-rule/

Chapter 2 — Notes

The quotation from *The Strange Career of Jim Crow* (New York: Oxford Univ. Press, 1957, is from page 8 of that edition.

The quotation from Terry Anderson's *The Pursuit of Fairness: A History of Affirmative Action* (New York: Oxford University Press, 2004), is from page 6 of that edition.

The quotation from *The Souls of Black Folk* (Greenwich, CT: Fawcett Publications,1961) is from page 133 of that edition.

That President Theodore Roosevelt approved of lynching in the case of rape is documented in my book, *Presidential Racism*, pp. 115 ff.

Examples of racist exclusions from higher education are contained in the state-by-state chapters beginning with Chapter 5.

W. E. B. Du Bois' statement about Vassar College is from *The Autobiography of W. E. B. DuBois* (New York: International Publishers, 1968), pages 137-138 of that edition.

The quotation from Woodrow Wilson is documented in my book, *Presidential Racism*, page 124.

Information about BiDil is contained in Jonathan Kahn's chapter, "BiDil and Racialized Medicine," ch. 7 of *Race and the Genetic Revolution: Science, Myth, and Culture*, ed. Sheldon Krimsky and Kathleen Sloan, pages 129 ff. More general information about racialized medicine is contained in "How Your Race Can Change your Medical Care," *Consumer Reports*, Dec., 2020, pp. 46 ff., and in "Covid-19 has shone a light on racial disparities in health," *The Economist*, Nov. 21, 2020, pp. 53 ff.

The cite for the quotation from the *Dred Scott* decision is *Dred Scott* v. *Sandford*, 60 U.S. 393, 407 (1857).

The origin of the concept of "race" was informed by Nancy D. Fortney, "The Anthropological Concept of Race," *Journal of Black Studies*, Vol.8, No.1, Sept., 1977, pp. 35 ff; Jacques Barzun, *Race: A Study in Superstition*; the three books listed below by Ashley Montagu; Johnston Greene, *The Negro in Colonial New England, 1620-1776*; Winthrop Jordan, *White Over Black: American Attitudes Toward the Negro, 1550-1812*; Jacqueline Jones, *A Dreadful Deceit: The Myth of Race from the Colonial Era to Obama's America*; and Peggy Pascoe,

What Comes Naturally: Miscegenation Law and the Making of Race in America.

The content of Chapter 2 is based on many various combinations of multiple sources listed below, personal experience and family history.

Chapter 2 — Sources

ACLU, "Voting Rights in Indian Country: A Special Report of the Voting Rights Project of the American Civil Liberties Union," 2009.

American Association of Physical Anthropologists, "Statement on Race and Racism" adopted March 27, 2019.

American Journal of Human Genetics, "ASHG Denounces Attempts to Link Genetics and Racial Supremacy,'" ASHG Perspective, Volume 103, Issue 5, p. 636, Nov. 01, 2018.

Anderson, Terry H., *The Pursuit of Fairness: A History of Affirmative Action* (New York: Oxford Univ. Press, 2004).

Barry, John M., *Roger Williams and the Creation of the American Soul* (New York: Viking, 2012).

Barzun, Jacques, *Race: A Study in Superstition* (New York: Harper & Row, 1965; originally published in 1937).

Blumrosen, Alfred W. & Ruth G. Blumrosen, *Slave Nation: How Slavery United the Colonies & Sparked the American Revolution* (Naperville, Illinois: Sourcebooks, 2005).

Brown v. Board of Education, 347 U.S. 483 (1954)

Buster, Greene B., *Brighter Sun* (New York: Pageant Press, 1954).

Coates, Ta-Nehisi, *Between the World and Me* (New York: Spiegel & Grau, 2015).

Consumer Reports, Dec., 2020, "How Your Race Can Change your Medical Care," pp. 46 ff.

Darwin, Charles, *The Descent of Man* (London: Penguin Books, 2004).

Davis, David Brion, *The Problem of Slavery in Western Culture* (Ithica, New York: Cornell Univ. Press, 1969).

De Beauvoir, Simone, *The Second Sex*, H. M. Parshley, trans & ed. (New York: Bantam Books, 1961; originally published in French in 1949).

Dennis, Michael, *Luther P. Jackson and a Life for Civil Rights* (Gainesville: Univ. Press of Florida, 2004).

Dobbs v. *Jackson Women's Health Organization*, 597 U.S. ____ (2022).

Dobzhansky, Theodosius, *Genetics and the Origin of Species* (New York: Columbia Univ. Press, 1st ed., 1937).

Douglass, Frederick, *Narrative of the Life of Frederick Douglass, An American Slave* (Garden City, New York: Doubleday, 1963).

Dray, Philip, "Breaking the silence about a lynching in the North," *Boston Globe*, June 2, 2022.

Dred Scott v. *Sandford*, 60 U.S. 393 (1856).

Du Bois, W. E. B., *Dusk of Dawn* (New York: Schocken Books, 1968; originally published in 1940).

Du Bois, W. E. B., *The Autobiography of W. E. B. DuBois* (New York: International Publishers, 1968).

Du Bois, W.E.B., *The Souls of Black Folk* (Greenwich, CT: Fawcett Publications,1961).

Dudziak, Mary L., *Cold War Civil Rights: Race and the Image of American Democracy* (Princeton, New Jersey: Princeton Univ. Press, paperback reissue 2011).

Eisler, Riane, *The Chalice and the Blade* (San Francisco: Harper & Row, 1988)

Estes, Kelli, *The Girl Who Wrote in Silk* (Naperville, Illinois: Sourcebooks, 2015).

Fortney, Nancy D., "The Anthropological Concept of Race," *Journal of Black Studies*, Vol.8, No.1, September., 1977.

Fredrickson, George M. *The Arrogance of Race: Historical Perspectives on Slavery, Racism, and Social Inequality* (Hanover, New Hampshire: Wesleyan Univ. Press, 1988).

Fredrickson, George M., *Racism: A Short History* (Princeton, New Jersey: Princeton Univ. Press, 2002).

Freire, Paulo, *Pedagogy of the Oppressed*, trans. M. B. Ramos (New York: Seabury Press, 1970).

Friedan, Betty, *The Feminine Mystique* (New York: Dell Publishing Co., 1963).

Graybill, Andrew R., *The Red and the White* (New York: Liveright Publishing, 2013).

Greene, Johnston, *The Negro in Colonial New England, 1620-1776* (New York: Columbia Univ. Press, 1942).

Hannah-Jones, Nikole, et. Al., editors, *The 1619 Project* (New York: One World, 2021).

Hernton, Calvin C., *Sex and Racism in America* (New York: Grove Press, 1965).

Hodge, John L., "Equality: Beyond Dualism and Oppression," Chapter 6 of *Anatomy of Racism*, ed. David Theo Goldberg (Minneapolis: Univ. of Minnesota Press, 1990), and sources cited therein.

Hodge, John L, *How We Are Our Enemy – And How to Stop: Our Unfinished Task of Fulfilling the Values of Democracy* (Jamaica Plain, Mass.: John L. Hodge, Publisher, 2011), and sources cited therein.

Hodge, John L, *Overcoming the Lie of "Race": A Personal, Philosophical, and Political Perspective*, Second Edition (Jamaica Plain, Mass.: John L. Hodge, Publisher, 2017), and sources cited therein.

Hodge, John L., *Presidential Racism: The Words of U.S. Presidents Since the Civil War, and an Essay: The Enduring Anti-Democratic Disease Afflicting Us – And Its Cure* (Jamaica Plain, Mass.: John L. Hodge, Publisher, 2020), and sources cited therein.

Hodge, John L., Donald K. Struckmann and Lynn Dorland Trost, *Cultural Bases of Racism and Group Oppression: An Examination of Traditional "Western" Concepts, Values and Institutional Structures Which Support Racism, Sexism and Elitism* (Berkeley, Calif.: Two Riders Press, 1975), and sources cited therein.

Part I and Part IV of this book are reprinted in *Race and Culture in America*, 3rd edition, ed. C. E. Jackson and E. J. Tolbert (Edina MN: Burgess International Group, 1989).

Hunt, Lynn, *Inventing Human Rights* (New York: W. W. Norton & Co., 2007).

Irving, Debby, *Waking Up White and Finding Myself in the Story of Race* (Cambridge, Mass: Elephant Room Press, 2014).

Jones, Jacqueline, *A Dreadful Deceit: The Myth of Race from the Colonial Era to Obama's America* (New York: Basic Books, 2013).

Jordan, Winthrop, *White Over Black: American Attitudes Toward the Negro, 1550-1812* (Baltimore: Penguin Books, 1969).

Kahn, Jonathan, "BiDil and Racialized Medicine," ch. 7 of *Race and the Genetic Revolution: Science, Myth, and Culture*, ed. Sheldon Krimsky and Kathleen Sloan (New York: Columbia Univ. Press, 2011).

Kluger, Richard, *Simple Justice: The History of* Brown v. Board of Education *and Black America's Struggle for Equality* (New York: Vintage Books, 2004).

Krimsky, Sheldon and Kathleen Sloan, ed., *Race and the Genetic Revolution: Science, Myth, and Culture* (New York: Columbia Univ. Press, 2011).

Loving v. Virginia, 388 U.S. 1 (1967).

McDonald, Laughlin, "The Voting Rights Act in Indian Country: South Dakota, A Case Study," 29 American Indian Law Review 43 (2004–2005).

Montagu, Ashley, "The Meaninglessness of the Anthropological Conception of Race," *The Journal of Heredity*, Vol. 23, 1941, pp. 243-247; originally published in Ashley Montagu, ed., *The Concept of Race*, p. 1.

Montagu, Ashley, ed., *The Concept of Race* (London: Collier Books, 1969).

Montagu, Ashley, *Man's Most Dangerous Myth: The Fallacy of Race*, 4th ed. (Cleveland: World Pub. Co., 1964); 1st ed. Originally published in 1942; sixth ed. (Lanham, Maryland: AltaMira Press, 1997).

Montell, Lynwood, "The Coe Ridge Colony: A Racial Island Disappears," *American Anthropologist*, Vol. 74, Issue 3, pp. 710 ff., 1972.

Montell, William Lynwood, *The Saga of Coe Ridge* (Knoxville: Univ. of Tennessee Press, 1970).

Morrison, Toni, *A Mercy* (New York: Alfred A. Knopf, 2008).

Oswalt, Wendell H., *This Land Was Theirs: A Study of the North American Indian* (New York: John Wiley & Sons, 1966).

Pääbo, Svante, *Neanderthal Man: In Search of Lost Genomes* (New York: Basic Books, 2014).

Partanen, Anu, *The Nordic Theory of Everything* (New York: HarperCollins, 2016).

Pascoe, Peggy, *What Comes Naturally: Miscegenation Law and the Making of Race in America* (New York: Oxford Univ. Press, 2009).

Plessy v. *Ferguson*, 163 U.S. 537 (1896).

Polanyi, Michael, *The Tacit Dimension* (Garden City, NY: Doubleday, 1967,

Pollitzer, William S. "The Physical Anthropology and Genetics of Marginal People of the Southeastern United States," *American Anthropologist*, Vol. 74, Issue 3, pp. 719 ff, 1972.

Rodney, Walter, *How Europe Underdeveloped Africa* (Washington, D.C.: Howard Univ. Press, 1974).

Roundtree, Helen C., *Pocahontas's People: The Powhatan "Indians" of Virginia Through Four Centuries* (Norman: Univ. of Oklahoma Press, 1989).

Sartre, Jean-Paul, *Anti-Semite and Jew*, trans. George J. Becker (New York: Schocken Books, 1965).

Seelye, Katherine Q., "Rhode island Church Taking Unusual Step to Illuminate Its Slavery Role," *The New York Times*, Aug. 24, 2015, p. A9.

Sharfstein, Daniel J., *The Invisible Line: A Secret History of Race in America* (New York: Penguin Group, 2011).

Shetterly, Margot Lee, *Hidden Figures: The American Dream and the Untold Story of the Black Women Mathematicians Who Helped Win the Space Race* (New York: William Morrow, 2016).

Shirt v. Hazeltine, U.S. District Court, District of South Dakota, 336 F. Supp. 2d 976 (D.S.D. 2004), 1018 – 1034.

Showboat, a play written by Oscar Hammerstein II based on a novel by Edna Ferber with music by Jerome Kern.

Somerset v. Stewart (1772), 98 ER 499; 12 Geo. 3.

Sternberg, Robert J., et al., "Intelligence, Race, and Genetics," *Race and the Genetic Revolution: Science, Myth, and Culture*, ed. Sheldon Krimsky and Kathleen Sloan (New York: Columbia Univ. Press, 2011).

Sykes, Byran, *DNA USA: A Genetic Portrait of America* (New York: Liveright Pub., 2012).

tenBroek, Jacobus, et al., *Prejudice, War and the Constitution* (Berkeley: Univ. of California Press, 1970).

The Economist, "Covid-19 has shone a light on racial disparities in health," Nov. 21, 2020, pp. 53 – 55.

The Economist, "Johnson: Snide and prejudice," June 13, 2020, p. 68.

Tilton, Robert S., *Pocahontas: The Evolution of an American Narrative* (New York: Cambridge Univ. Press, 1994).

Weatherford, Jack, *The Secret History of the Mongol Queens: How the Daughters of Genghis Khan Rescued His Empire* (New York: Crown Publishers, 2010).

Weinstein, Rhona S., *Reaching Higher: The Power of Expectations in Schooling* (Cambridge, Mass.: Harvard Univ. Press, 2002).

Whitehead, Alfred North, *Science and the Modern World* (New York: Mentor Books, 1959; originally published in 1925).

Whitman, James Q, *Hitler's American Model: The United States and the Making of Nazi Race Law* (Princeton: Princeton Univ. Press, 2017).

Winch, Julie, *Between Slavery and Freedom* (Lanham, Maryland: Rowland & Littlefield, 2014).

Wood, Betty, *The Origins of American Slavery* (New York: Hill and Wang, 1997).

Woodward, C. Vann, *The Strange Career of Jim Crow* (New York: Oxford Univ. Press, 1957.)

Yudell II, Michael, "A Short History of the Race Concept," *Race and the Genetic Revolution: Science, Myth, and Culture*, ed. Sheldon Krimsky and Kathleen Sloan (New York: Columbia Univ. Press, 2011.

Zornow, William Frank, *Kansas: A History of the Jayhawk State* (Norman: Univ. of Oklahoma Press, 1957).

Online sources:

"How Literacy Became a Powerful Weapon in the Fight to End Slavery," Jan. 29. 2021:
https://www.history.com/news/nat-turner-rebellion-literacy-slavery

"'It's now come to our doorstep': Librarians find themselves at the center of increasingly bitter culture wars," Feb. 5, 2023:
https://www.bostonglobe.com/2023/02/05/metro/librarians-center-culture-war/

"Libraries face increased attempts to ban books," Sept. 23, 2022:
https://www.bostonglobe.com/2022/09/23/metro/libraries-face-increased-attempts-ban-books/?s_campaign=breakingnews:newsletter

"New study finds white male minority rule dominates US," May 26, 2021:
https://thehill.com/changing-america/respect/diversity-inclusion/555503-new-study-finds-white-male-minority-rule/

"No Surprise Here: The Most Recent Wave of Book Bans Includes More Black Authors Than Ever," Jan. 9, 2022:
https://www.theroot.com/no-surprise-here-the-most-recent-wave-of-book-bans-inc-1848328977?utm_source=theroot_newsletter&utm_medium=email&utm_campaign=2022-01-09

"System Failure: What the 2020 Primary Elections revealed about our democracy," May, 2021:

https://wholeads.us/research/system-failure-2020-primary-elections/

"*The 1619 Project* and the Long Battle Over U.S. History," Nov. 9, 2021:
https://www.nytimes.com/2021/11/09/magazine/1619-project-us-history.html

Chapter 3 — Notes and Sources

Mr. Knudsen's opinion is available online through the link in this article: https://dojmt.gov/attorney-general-knudsen-issues-binding-opinion-on-critical-race-theory/ .

Other sources include:

Dobbs v. *Jackson Women's Health Organization*, 597 U.S. ____ (2022).

Hodge, John L, *How We Are Our Enemy — And How to Stop: Our Unfinished Task of Fulfilling the Values of Democracy*, Chapter 6 (Jamaica Plain, Mass.: John L. Hodge, Publisher, 2011).

Hodge, John L., "The Enduring Anti-Democratic Disease Afflicting Us — And Its Cure," contained in Part I of *Presidential Racism: The Words of U.S. Presidents Since the Civil War* (Jamaica Plain, Mass.: John L. Hodge, Publisher, 2020).

Loving v. *Virginia*, 388 U.S. 1 (1967).

Plessy v. *Ferguson*, 163 U.S. 537 (1896).

The Constitution of the United States.

Chapters 4 to 19 — Notes

Citations to state laws and references to official state websites are contained in the text and not repeated here.

Chapter 4 — Notes and Sources

The quotation from *The Economist* columnist is from "Johnson: Snide and prejudice," *The Economist*, June 13, 2020, p. 68.

The book, *The 1619 Project* (New York: One World, 2021), is edited by Nikole Hannah-Jones and several others.

Mr. Knudsen's opinion is available online through the link in this article: https://dojmt.gov/attorney-general-knudsen-issues-binding-opinion-on-critical-race-theory/ .

Among the sources that treat the "barbarians" as people is Malcolm Todd's *The Everyday Life of The Barbarians: Goths, Franks and Vandals* (New York: G. P. Putnam's Sons, 1972).

Other sources include:

Hodge, John L, "Understanding Merit and the Need to Replace 'Affirmative Action,'" Chapter 9 of *Overcoming the Lie of "Race": A Personal, Philosophical, and Political Perspective,* Second Edition, (Jamaica Plain, Mass.: John L. Hodge, Publisher, 2017). The quotation is from p. 113.

The Economist, "A self-repressing society," May 14, 2022, p. 42.

The Economist, "The Communist Party: Control the present, control the past," Nov. 6, 2021, pp. 37-38.

Chapters 5 to 19 — Notes and Sources

In the state-by-state chapters, the thumbs-down hands are the author's estimates of the severity of each state's laws, with five thumbs-down indicating the most severe.

Citations to state laws and references to official state websites are contained in the text and not repeated here.

Online sources common to many of these chapters:

"2020 Population and Housing State Data," Aug. 12, 2021: https://www.census.gov/library/visualizations/interactive/2020-population-and-housing-state-data.html

"As Confederate monuments come down, some states have laws that protect their removal." July 10, 2020: https://www.thetelegraph.com/news/article/As-Confederate-monuments-come-down-some-states-15382654.php#:~:text=The%20law%20states%20it%20is,United%20States%20and%20the%20Confederacy

"Banned in the USA: The Growing Movement to Censor Books in Schools," Sept. 19, 2022: https://pen.org/report/banned-usa-growing-movement-to-censor-books-in-schools/

"Black Population Percentage (by State)," undated: https://www.indexmundi.com/facts/united-states/quick-facts/florida/black-population-percentage#map

"Confederate Memorial Day," undated: https://en.wikipedia.org/wiki/Confederate_Memorial_Day

"Critical race theory" is being weaponised. What's the fuss about?" July 14, 2022: https://www.economist.com/interactive/united-states/2022/07/14/critical-race-theory-is-being-weaponised-whats-the-fuss-about

"Jim Crow Laws: North Dakota, Ohio and Oklahoma," undated: https://americansall.org/legacy-story-group/jim-crow-laws-north-dakota-ohio-and-oklahoma

"Map: Where Critical Race Theory Is Under Attack," Mar. 13, 2023: https://www.edweek.org/policy-politics/map-where-critical-race-theory-is-under-attack/2021/06

"Number of books titles banned in school classrooms and libraries in the United States from July 1, 2021 to June 30, 2022, by state," Nov. 2, 2022: https://www.statista.com/statistics/1310288/school-book-bans-us-by-state/

"Ratification Info State by State," undated: https://www.equalrightsamendment.org/era-ratification-map#:~:text=The%2015%20states%20that%20did,Carolina%2C%20Utah%2C%20and%20Virginia

"States with the toughest abortion laws have the weakest maternal supports, data shows," Aug. 18, 2022:

https://www.npr.org/2022/08/18/1111344810/abortion-ban-states-social-safety-net-health-outcomes

"The 50 most banned books in America," Nov. 10, 2022: https://www.cbsnews.com/pictures/the-50-most-banned-books-in-america/

"The Equal Rights Amendment Explained," Jan. 23, 2020: https://www.brennancenter.org/our-work/research-reports/equal-rights-amendment-explained

"The Equal Rights Amendment: Recent Developments," Apr. 25, 2022: https://crsreports.congress.gov/product/pdf/LSB/LSB10731

"The First Black Students Admitted to 15 Prestigious U.S. Universities, and Their Stories," Feb 16, 2013: https://www.complex.com/pop-culture/2013/02/the-first-black-students-admitted-to-15-prestigious-us-universities-and-their-stories

"Where Is Abortion Legal? A State-by-State Guide to Current Laws," Jan. 23, 2023: https://www.nbcwashington.com/news/national-international/where-is-abortion-legal-a-state-by-state-guide-to-current-laws/3259835/

Chapter 5 (Texas) — Sources

Baumgartner, Alice L., *South to Freedom: Runaway Slaves to Mexico and the Road to the Civil War* (New York: Basic Books, 2020).

Carroll, Mark M., *Homesteads Ungovernable: Families, Sex, Race and the Law in Frontier Texas 1823 - 1860* (Austin, Texas: Univ. of Texas Press, 2001).

Online sources:

"A Texas lawmaker is targeting 850 books that he says could make students feel uneasy," Oct. 28, 2022:
https://www.npr.org/2021/10/28/1050013664/texas-lawmaker-matt-krause-launches-inquiry-into-850-books

"Diversity, Equity and Inclusion," Oct. 19, 2021:
https://www.utexas.edu/about/diversity-equity-and-inclusion

"List of Confederate monuments and memorials," last edited on February 21, 2023:
https://en.wikipedia.org/wiki/List_of_Confederate_monuments_and_memorials#:~:text=Of%20the%20more%20than%201503,%2C%20Virginia%2C%20or%20North%20Carolina

"Texas has banned more books than any other state, new report shows," Sept. 19, 2022:
https://www.texastribune.org/2022/09/19/texas-book-bans/

"Texas has more than 180 public symbols of the Confederacy. Explore them here," Aug. 22, 2017:
https://www.texastribune.org/2017/08/21/texas-has-second-most-public-symbols-confederacy-nation/

"Texas leads among 26 states with book bans, free speech group says," Apr. 7, 2022:

https://www.cnn.com/2022/04/07/us/book-bans-pen-america-analysis/index.html

"The Precursors," udated:
https://diversity.utexas.edu/integration/the-precursors/

"Why Texas Still Celebrates Confederate Heroes Day," July 3, 2020:
https://www.texasmonthly.com/news-politics/texas-confederate-heroes-day-abolish/

Chapter 6 (Florida) — Sources

Baumgartner, Alice L., *South to Freedom: Runaway Slaves to Mexico and the Road to the Civil War* (New York: Basic Books, 2020).

Paulson, Darryl and Paul Hawkes, "Desegregating The University of Florida Law School: Virgil Hawkins v. The Florida Board of Control," Florida State University Law Review, Vol. 12, Issue 1 (Spring 1984).

"Florida's woke wars," *The Economist*, Jan. 28, 2023, pp. 22-23.

Online sources:

"Andrew Jackson's promise of 'good government' for Pensacola was a hollow one," J. Richard Cohen, Mar. 14, 2021:
https://www.pnj.com/story/opinion/2021/03/14/andrew-jackson-promise-good-government-pensacola-florida-hollow-one/6929967002/

"Andrew Jackson 1767-1845: A brief biography," undated: http://www.let.rug.nl/usa/biographies/andrew-jackson/eviction-of-indians-and-taking-of-florida.php

"As Confederate monuments come down, some states have laws that protect their removal," July 10, 2020: https://www.thetelegraph.com/news/article/As-Confederate-monuments-come-down-some-states-15382654.php#:~:text=The%20law%20states%20it%20is,United%20States%20and%20the%20Confederacy

"The Gullah: Rice, Slavery, and the Sierra Leone-American Connection," Joseph A. Opala, undated: https://glc.yale.edu/sites/default/files/files/Black%20Seminoles%20.pdf

"UF Diversity Metrics," undated: https://cdo.ufl.edu/strategic-initiatives/metrics/#:~:text=The%20race%20and%20ethnicity%20of,American%20Indian%20or%20Alaska%20Native

"Who We Are," undated: https://afam.clas.ufl.edu/overview/#:~:text=Hawkins%20eventually%20received%20his%20J.D.,university's%20first%20African%20American%20student.

Chapter 7 (Georgia) — Note and Sources

The quotation at the beginning is from "Largest Slave Sale in Georgia History," June 16, 2014: https://georgiahistory.com/ghmi_marker_updated/largest-slave-sale-in-georgia-history/

Additional online sources:

"As Confederate monuments come down, some states have laws that protect their removal," July 10, 2020:
https://www.thetelegraph.com/news/article/As-Confederate-monuments-come-down-some-states-15382654.php#:~:text=The%20law%20states%20it%20is,United%20States%20and%20the%20Confederacy

"Civil War Memorial," undated:
https://gallivantertours.com/savannah/statues-monuments/confederate-monument/

"Fanny Kemble and Pierce Butler," undated:
https://www.pbs.org/wgbh/aia/part4/4p1569.html

"Georgia Secedes from Union," undated:
https://www.todayingeorgiahistory.org/tih-georgia-day/georgia-secedes-from-union/#:~:text=Heated%20debate%20led%20to%20an,cause%20for%20dissolving%20the%20Union

"The Weeping Time," by Kristopher Monroe, July 10, 2014:
https://www.theatlantic.com/business/archive/2014/07/the-weeping-time/374159

"UGA Student Racial-Ethnic Demographics," undated:
https://www.collegefactual.com/colleges/university-of-georgia/student-life/diversity/chart-ethnic-diversity.html

Chapter 8 (Virginia) — Sources

Online sources:
"An Act to amend the act concerning slaves, free negroes and mulattoes (April 7, 1831)," undated:
https://encyclopediavirginia.org/entries/an-act-to-amend-the-act-concerning-slaves-free-negroes-and-mulattoes-april-7-1831/

"Enrollment by Race & Ethnicity." Undated:
https://datausa.io/profile/university/university-of-virginia-main-campus#:~:text=1%2C661-,The%20enrolled%20student%20population%20at%20University%20of%20Virginia%2DMain%20Campus,Hawaiian%20or%20Other%20Pacific%20Islanders

"Gov. Youngkin sets up tip line to report 'divisive' teaching practices," Jan. 26, 2022:
https://www.nbc12.com/2022/01/25/gov-youngkin-sets-up-tip-line-report-divisive-teaching-practices/

"James Madison," undated:
https://slavery.princeton.edu/stories/james-madison#:~:text=James%20Madison%2C%20Princeton%20alumnus%20and,to%20the%20White%20House%2C%20and

"Reported number of slaves owned by U.S. presidents who served from 1789 to 1877," June 21, 2022:
https://www.statista.com/statistics/1121963/slaves-owned-by-us-presidents/#:~:text=Of%20the%20U.S.'%20first%20twelve,until%20all%20slaves%20were%20freed

"The 1619 Landing—Virginia's First Africans Report & FAQs," undated:
https://hampton.gov/3580/The-1619-Landing-Report-FAQs#:~:text=In%20late%20August%2C%201619%2C%2020,Virginia%20with%20additional%20enslaved%20Africans

"U.Va.'s First African-American Undergraduate Leads Engineering School Panel on Diversity," Jan. 26, 2011:
https://news.virginia.edu/content/uvas-first-african-american-undergraduate-leads-engineering-school-panel-diversity

"Virginia Governor Glenn Youngkin's Anti-Critical Race Theory Tip Line," Aug. 8, 2022:
https://www.americanoversight.org/investigation/virginia-governor-glenn-youngkins-anti-critical-race-theory-tip-line

"When did Virginia join the Confederacy?" Sept. 19, 2019:
https://richmond.com/special-section/when-did-virginia-join-the-confederacy/article_f52cda34-4e4f-534b-a9fd-ff6cc17ef9cc.html#:~:text=The%20Virginia%20Convention%20voted%20to,the%20Confederate%20States%20of%20America

Chapter 9 (Tennessee) — Sources

Online sources:

"Confederate statutes and monuments in Tennessee," July 30, 2020:

https://www.tennessean.com/picture-gallery/news/2020/07/30/confederate-statues-and-monuments-tennessee/5349270002/

"Educator Diversity State Profile: Tennessee," July 27, 2022: https://edtrust.org/resource/educator-diversity-state-profile-tennessee/
"Ku Klux Klan," Mar. 1, 2018: https://tennesseeencyclopedia.net/entries/ku-klux-klan/

"Ku Klux Klan," Feb. 4, 2022: https://www.history.com/topics/19th-century/ku-klux-klan

"Mapping Tennessee Education: Student demographics in school year 2019-2020," undated: https://comptroller.tn.gov/content/dam/cot/orea/advanced-search/2021/Studentdemographics.pdf

"Tennessee Demographics & Diversity," undated: https://www.collegesimply.com/colleges/tennessee/the-university-of-tennessee/students/

"Tennessee Population 2023," undated: https://worldpopulationreview.com/states/tennessee-population

"UT Integrates," Sept. 20, 2019: https://history.utk.edu/ut-integrates/#:~:text=Theotis%20Robinson%20Jr.%2C%20Charles%20Blair,black%20undergraduates%20in%20January%201961.

Chapter 10 (South Carolina) — Sources

Online sources:

"Civil War Glass Negatives and Related Prints," undated: https://www.loc.gov/collections/civil-war-glass-negatives/articles-and-essays/time-line-of-the-civil-war/1861/#:~:text=The%20secession%20of%20South%20Carolina,the%20Confederate%20States%20of%20America

"Diversity Data," undated: https://sc.edu/about/offices_and_divisions/diversity_equity_and_inclusion/diversity_data/index.php

"Establishing Slavery in the Lowcountry," undated: https://ldhi.library.cofc.edu/exhibits/show/africanpassageslowcountryadapt/sectionii_introduction

"Horry County Board Bans CRT Despite It Not Being Taught in Classrooms," Aug. 23, 2022: https://www.newsweek.com/horry-county-board-bans-crt-despite-it-not-being-taught-classrooms-1736234

"In Charleston, Black history is being told through a new lens," June 24, 2021: https://www.nationalgeographic.com/travel/article/in-charleston-black-history-is-being-told-through-a-new-lens

"South Carolina Middle School Removes Book on Anti-Racism From Library," Oct. 25, 2022: https://ncac.org/news/south-carolina-school-removes-book-anti-racism

"South Carolina Population 2023," undated:

https://worldpopulationreview.com/states/south-carolina-population

"South Carolina Middle School Removes Book on Anti-Racism From Library," undated:
https://ncac.org/news/south-carolina-school-removes-book-anti-racism

"South Carolina's racist history," June 23, 2015:
https://www.baltimoresun.com/opinion/op-ed/bs-ed-schaller-0624-20150623-column.html

Chapter 11 (Alabama) — Sources

The Economist, "The girl who loved reading," March 26, 2022, p. 86.

Online sources:

"Ala. Admin. Code r. 290-040-040-.02," current as of Feb. 28, 2023:
https://casetext.com/regulation/alabama-administrative-code/title-290-alabama-state-board-of-education/chapter-290-040-040-audits-and-management-services/section-290-040-040-02-certain-teaching-techniques?searchWithin=true&listingIndexId=alabama-administrative-code.title-290-alabama-state-board-of-education&q=race&type=regulation&sort=relevance&p=1#:~:text=Certain%20Teaching%20Techniques-,Ala.%20Admin.%20Code%20r.%20290%2D040%2D040%2D.02,-Download%20PDF

"Alabama Board of Education resolution bans critical race theory-type teachings, Aug. 12, 2021: https://www.montgomeryadvertiser.com/story/news/education/2021/08/12/alabama-board-education-bans-critical-race-theory-teaching-public-schools/5543324001/

"Alabama State Board of Education Resolution Declaring the Preservation of Intellectual Freedom And Nondiscrimination in Alabama's Public Schools," Aug. 12, 2021: https://www.alabamaachieves.org/wp-content/uploads/2021/08/ALSBOE-Resolution-Declaring-the-Preservation-of-Intellectual-Freedom-and-Non-Discrimination-in-AL-Public-Schools.pdf

"Alabama state school board passes resolution banning Critical Race Theory," Aug. 16, 2021: https://www.alreporter.com/2021/08/16/alabama-state-school-board-passes-resolution-banning-critical-race-theory/

"Did Kay Ivey ban 'Critical Race Theory' from Alabama schools in October 2021?" Nov. 1, 2021: https://www.lmax.com/blog/business-and-technology/2021/11/01/did-kay-ivey-ban-critical-race-theory-from-alabama-schools-in-october-2021/

"States meet to form Confederacy," updated Feb. 1, 2022: https://www.history.com/this-day-in-history/states-meet-to-form-confederacy

"The University of Alabama: Students by Race/Ethnicity," undated:

https://oira.ua.edu/factbook/reports/student-enrollment/fall-term/students-by-race-and-ethnicity/202140.html

Chapter 12 (Kentucky) — Sources

Berea College v. *Kentucky*, 211 U.S. 45 (1908).

Online sources:

"A House Divided: Civil War Kentucky," Dec. 21, 2021: https://www.battlefields.org/learn/articles/house-divided-civil-war-kentucky#:~:text=On%20November%2018%2C%20200%20delegates,Confederacy%20as%20a%2013th%20state.

"Desegregation of UK," undated: https://explorekyhistory.ky.gov/items/show/145#:~:text=Lyman%20Johnson%3A%20Lyman%20Johnson%20fought,of%20the%20University%20of%20Kentucky

"Jackson, John Henry," March 6, 2023: https://libraryguides.berea.edu/johnhenryjackson#:~:text=John%20Henry%20Jackson&text=He%20graduated%20from%20Berea%20College,He%20was%20awarded%20an%20A.M.

"Kentucky Demographics & Diversity," undated: https://www.collegesimply.com/colleges/kentucky/university-of-kentucky/students/

"Kentucky State University," undated:

https://www.kysu.edu/search/index.php?query=john+jackson

"Notable Kentucky African Americans Database: Jackson, John Henry," April 23, 2021:
https://nkaa.uky.edu/nkaa/items/show/403

"Our Inclusive History: From 1855 to Today," undated:
https://www.berea.edu/about/1855-to-today/

"Slavery Laws in Old Kentucky," undated:
https://explorekyhistory.ky.gov/items/show/180

"University of Kentucky," undated:
https://datausa.io/profile/university/university-of-kentucky

Chapter 13 (Oklahoma) — Sources

Online sources:

"Chronological History: University of Oklahoma," undated:
https://ou.edu/content/dam/irr/docs/Fact%20Book/fact-book-2020/20_1_07_chron.pdf

"FAQ: What we know about teaching since Oklahoma's so-called critical race theory ban went into effect," undated:
https://stateimpact.npr.org/oklahoma/2022/09/08/faq-what-we-know-about-teaching-since-oklahomas-so-called-critical-race-theory-ban-went-into-effect/

"Oklahoma joins Union as the 46th state, Nov. 16, 1907," Nov. 16, 2015:
https://www.politico.com/story/2015/11/oklahoma-joins-union-as-the-46th-state-215767#:~:text=On%20this%20day%20in%201907,Territory%20and%20the%20Oklahoma%20Territory

"Oklahoma's Embrace of the White Racial Identity," May, 2021:
https://www.okbar.org/barjournal/may-2021/johnson-juarez-2021/

"OU Demographics & Diversity," undated:
https://www.collegesimply.com/colleges/oklahoma/university-of-oklahoma-norman-campus/students/

"Stitt signs controversial bill censoring teachings on race, gender," May 7, 2021:
https://www.oklahoman.com/story/news/2021/05/07/oklahoma-gov-stitt-signs-bill-censoring-race-gender-school-curriculum/4989720001/

"The Encyclopedia of Oklahoma History and Culture: Segregation," undated:
https://www.okhistory.org/publications/enc/entry.php?entry=SE006

"The Encyclopedia of Oklahoma History and Culture: Slavery," undated:
https://www.okhistory.org/publications/enc/entry.php?entry=SL003

"The story of George W. McLaren, the First Black man to be admitted to the University of Oklahoma," undated:

https://ng.opera.news/ng/en/education/78a7ae3ced820
5fe3bff9928f4ea1ddc

"Tulsa massacre: centennial of white mob rampage to be commemorated in Oklahoma," May 30, 2021:
https://www.theguardian.com/us-news/2021/may/30/tulsa-race-massacre-100th-anniversary-oklahoma

"Tulsa Race Massacre," May 24, 2022:
https://www.history.com/topics/roaring-twenties/tulsa-race-massacre#:~:text=During%20the%20Tulsa%20Race%20Massacre,Greenwood%20neighborhood%20of%20Tulsa%2C%20Oklahoma

Chapter 14 (Iowa) — Sources

Online sources:

"Black students in Grinnell call for action against racist harassment," Oct. 26, 2022:
https://www.iowapublicradio.org/ipr-news/2022-10-26/black-students-in-grinnell-call-for-action-against-racist-harassment

"Black students at Grinnell College speak out about racist event," Oct. 25, 2022:
https://www.weareiowa.com/article/news/education/racist-incidents-grinnell-college/524-5f955f86-a380-486b-98fb-7691421eb5c0

"Critical Thinking," undated:

https://www.ames-deserves-better.com/critical-thinking/

"Racism and Its Impact," June 6, 2022:
https://www.iowapbs.org/shows/telling-our-own-story/episode/7718/racism-and-its-impact

"Racist slurs, threats and disparities: Why Iowa City high school students walked out of class Friday," Nov. 22, 2021:
https://littlevillagemag.com/iowa-city-high-school-student-walk-out-racism/

"Resolution in Opposition to Racist Incidents Occurring at Iowa State University and in Support of Students Affected by Them," undated:
https://www.facsen.iastate.edu/sites/default/files/uploads/19-20%20Docket%20Calendar/19-8%20Resolution%20Opposition%20to%20Racist%20Incident%20at%20ISU.pdf

Chapter 15 (Arkansas) — Sources

Online sources:

"African Americans," undated:
https://encyclopediaofarkansas.net/entries/african-americans-407/

"Arkansas Demographics & Diversity," undated:
https://www.collegesimply.com/colleges/arkansas/university-of-arkansas/students/

"Arkansas governor allows bill targeting critical race theory in state agencies to become law," May 3, 2021:
https://thehill.com/homenews/state-watch/551609-arkansas-governor-allows-bill-targeting-critical-race-theory-in-state/#:~:text=The%20legislation%20bars%20state%20agencies,is%20an%20inherently%20racist%20nation

"Arkansas secedes from the Union, May 6, 1861," May 5, 2017:
https://www.politico.com/story/2017/05/05/arkansas-secedes-from-the-union-may-6-1861-238036#:~:text=On%20this%20day%20in%201861,the%20Confederate%20States%20of%20America.

"Executive Order to Prohibit Indoctrination and Critical Race Theory in Schools," undated:
https://governor.arkansas.gov/executive_orders/executive-order-to-prohibit-indoctrination-and-critical-race-theory-in-schools/

"History of the University of Arkansas," undated:
https://www.uark.edu/about/history.php

"Little Rock Nine," undated:
https://www.history.com/topics/black-history/central-high-school-integration

Chapter 16 (New Hampshire) — Sources

Online sources:

"Commentary: Does systemic racism exist in New Hampshire?" by Dan Weeks, et. al., June 2, 2021:
https://newhampshirebulletin.com/2021/06/02/commentary-does-systemic-racism-exist-in-new-hampshire/

"'Divisive concepts' law makes a splash, and its ripples spread beyond education," Sept. 29, 2022:
https://www.nhbr.com/divisive-concepts-law-makes-a-splash-and-its-ripples-spread-beyond-education/#:~:text=The%20new%20law%20prohibits%20teaching,racist%2C%20sexist%20or%20otherwise%20prejudiced

FAQ: Talking & Teaching About Racism in Schools," undated:
https://www.aclu-nh.org/en/faq-talking-teaching-about-racism-schools

"Frequently Asked Questions: New discriminatory practice prohibitions applicable to k-12 educational programs," undated:
https://www.doj.nh.gov/civil-rights/documents/faq-educational-programs.pdf

"New Center for Justice and Equity targets systemic racism in New Hampshire," Sept. 29, 2022:
https://www.nhbr.com/new-center-for-justice-and-equity-targets-systemic-racism-in-new-hampshire/

"NH Governor Condemns Tweet Offering a 'Bounty' on Teachers," Nov. 18, 2021:
https://www.nbcboston.com/news/local/nh-governor-condemns-tweet-offering-a-bounty-on-teachers/2570297/

"Right to Freedom from Discrimination in Public Workplaces and Education," undated:
https://www.education.nh.gov/who-we-are/deputy-commissioner/office-of-governance/right-to-freedom-from-discrimination

"Slavery in New Hampshire: Profitable godliness to racial consciousness," by Jody R. Fernald, Winter, 2007:
https://scholars.unh.edu/cgi/viewcontent.cgi?article=1067&context=thesis

Chapter 17 (Montana) — Notes and Sources

Montana Democratic Party, et. al. v. Jacobsen, Montana Thirteenth Judicial District Court Yellowstone County, Case No.: DV 21-0451.

Mr. Knudsen's opinion is available online through the link in this article: https://dojmt.gov/attorney-general-knudsen-issues-binding-opinion-on-critical-race-theory/ .

Additional online sources:

"2021 Montana Laws That Limit Native Voter Participation (Western Native Voice V. Jacobsen)," undated:
https://narf.org/cases/2021-montana-voter-laws/

"Attorney General Knudsen Issues Binding Opinion on Critical Race Theory," May 27, 2021:
https://dojmt.gov/attorney-general-knudsen-issues-binding-opinion-on-critical-race-theory/

"Bordertown Discrimination in Montana," May, 2019:
https://www.usccr.gov/files/pubs/2019/05-29-Bordertown-Discrimination-Montana.pdf

"Early history of African-Americans in Montana," Nov. 3, 2015:
https://www.greatfallstribune.com/story/life/2015/11/03/history-african-americans-montana/75127366/

"Harassment," undated:
https://www.eeoc.gov/harassment#:~:text=Harassment%20becomes%20unlawful%20where%201,intimidating%2C%20hostile%2C%20or%20abusive

Chapter 18 (South Dakota) — Sources

Rosebud Sioux Tribe, et. al. v. *Barnett*, U.S. District Court, South Dakota Western Division, Case 5:20-cv-05058-LLP (May 26. 2022).

Shirt v. *Hazeltine*, U.S. District Court, South Dakota Central Division, Civ. 01-3032-KES 2004 DSD 18 (Sept. 15, 2004).

Online sources:

"A South Dakota hotel denied service to Native Americans, lawsuit says," Mar. 25, 2022:

https://www.cnn.com/2022/03/25/us/south-dakota-hotel-lawsuit-native-americans/index.html

"American Indian Children Are Facing Racial Discrimination in the Classroom," Dec. 2022: https://ndkidscount.org/American-indian-children-are-facing-racial-discrimination-in-the-classroom

"Dakota Territory and Slavery," May 27, 2009: https://news.prairiepublic.org/show/dakota-datebook-archive/2022-05-21/dakota-territory-and-slavery

"Federal Court Rules South Dakota Violated Voting Rights of Native Americans," https://www.aclu.org/other/federal-court-rules-south-dakota-violated-voting-rights-native-americans

"In South Dakota, Native Americans face numerous obstacles to voting," Oct. 29, 2020: https://publicintegrity.org/politics/elections/us-polling-places/in-south-dakota-native-americans-face-numerous-obstacles-to-voting/

"Native Americans Confront Racism in South Dakota," May 28, 2022: https://www.voanews.com/a/native-americans-confront-racism-in-south-dakota/6590488.html

"South Dakota Voter Registration (Rosebud Sioux Tribe v. Barnett)," undated: https://narf.org/cases/south-dakota-voter-registration/

"State of South Dakota Office of the Governor Executive Order 2021-11," July 29, 2021:

https://sdsos.gov/general-information/executive-actions/executive-orders/assets/2021-11.PDF

Chapter 19 (North Dakota) — Sources

Online sources:

"American Indian Children Are Facing Racial Discrimination in the Classroom," Dec. 2022:
https://ndkidscount.org/American-indian-children-are-facing-racial-discrimination-in-the-classroom

"Dakota Territory and Slavery," May 27, 2009:
https://news.prairiepublic.org/show/dakota-datebook-archive/2022-05-21/dakota-territory-and-slavery

"Indigenous nations sue North Dakota over 'sickening' gerrymandering," Feb. 21, 2022:
https://www.theguardian.com/us-news/2022/feb/21/native-american-tribes-sue-north-dakota-gerrymandering

"Native American Justice Issues in North Dakota," 1978:
https://www.ojp.gov/ncjrs/virtual-library/abstracts/native-american-justice-issues-north-dakota

"ND State Department of Instruction: Critical Race Theory," Sept. 9, 2022:
https://www.kxnet.com/news/state-news/nd-state-department-of-instruction-critical-race-theory/

"North Dakota," Aug. 21, 2018:

https://www.history.com/topics/us-states/north-dakota#:~:text=The%20land%20that%20today%20makes,the%20Dakota%20Territory%20in%201861

"North Dakota Voter ID Law (Spirit Lake Tribe v. Jaeger)," undated:
https://narf.org/cases/spirit-lake-tribe-v-jaeger/

"One Man, No Vote: How Native Americans in North Dakota Lost the Right to Vote and Fought for Its Return," Apr. 29, 2020:
http://uchicagogate.com/articles/2020/4/29/one-man-no-vote-how-native-americans-north-dakota-lost-right-vote-and-fought-its-return/

"Spirit Lake Tribe et al., v. Alvin J eger," Oct. 30, 2018:
https://latino.ucla.edu/research/spirit-lake-tribe-et-al-v-alvin-jaeger/

Chapter 20 — Notes and Sources

This chapter is based on a combination of my life experiences and numerous resources, including the previous chapters and preface of this book and the sources listed for them.

Epilogue — Notes and Sources

The Epilogue is based on family history, my life experiences, and numerous resources, including the chapters and preface of this book and the sources listed for them.

INDEX

A

Abraham, Yvonne, 66
affirmative action, 18, 81
Africa, Africans, 8, 12, 21, 29, 32, 34, 36, 38, 54, 91, 118, 155, 175, 189, 194, 198, 201
Alabama, 109, 110, 111, 192, 193
  health care, 32, 160, 161
discomfort, 20, 37, 51, 53, 75, 97, 106, 120, 126, 141, 146
discrimination, 13, 57, 119, 120, 121, 136, 138, 200
American Association of Physical Anthropologists, 132, 169
American Journal of Human Genetics, 39, 169
American Revolution, 3, 5, 33, 169
Amsterdam, 7
Anderson, Terry H., 28
anthropology, 36, 156
antisemitism, 7, 42, 152, 153
apartheid, 8, 27
Aristotle, 14
Arkansas, 129, 130, 198, 199
Asians, 12, 17, 18, 20, 40, 52, 141

B

Bacon, Francis, 7
Barzun, Jacques, 37, 168, 169
Beethoven, 160
Berea College, 114, 115, 158, 194
Bill of Rights, 7, 34
Black women mathematicians, 21
Brahms, 152
Brecht, Bertolt, prior to p. 1
British colonies in America, 3, 5, 33, 54, 87
Brown v. Board of Education, 28, 30, 31, 44, 68, 79, 88, 95, 96, 103, 115, 117, 123, 164, 169, 173

C

China, 4, 61
Civil Rights Act of 1964, 31, 93, 144
Civil War, 4, 12, 27, 29, 31, 33, 34, 35, 47, 68, 73, 87, 95, 114, 115, 118, 119, 124, 130, 133, 138, 144, 162, 163, 166, 172, 179, 183, 185, 187, 190, 194
Coates, Ta-Nehisi, 94
colonies, 3, 5, 7, 16, 19, 29, 33, 36, 37, 145, 165
colorblindness, 24, 55
Confederacy, 31, 68, 69, 78, 88, 91, 95, 103, 109, 114, 118, 129, 184, 189, 193, 194
critical race theory, 2, 13, 21, 45, 48, 51, 55, 62, 63, 66, 84, 92, 94, 107, 110, 111, 112, 136, 139, 149, 150, 191, 192, 195, 198

D

Darwin, Charles, 37, 170
Declaration of Independence, 13, 33, 34, 84, 115, 145, 165
democracy, 1, 2, 3, 8, 9, 11, 36, 40, 145, 161, 178
Descartes, Rene, 7, 163
disability, people with, 47, 130, 134, 135
discipline, punishment, 60, 70, 72, 75, 83, 107, 122, 135
discrimination, 13, 29, 79, 81, 83, 115, 144, 200, 202, 203
divisive concepts, 88, 89, 92, 93, 108, 130, 145, 146, 147, 188, 199
Dobbs v. *Jackson Women's Health Organization*, 46, 179
Dred Scott v. *Sandford*, 34, 35, 45, 168, 171
Du Bois, W. E. B, 20, 28, 30, 168, 171

E

Edsall, Thomas B., 86
education, 12, 13, 15, 30, 57, 58, 66, 88, 96, 100, 110, 111, 114, 115, 121, 124 - 126, 130, 135, 157 - 159, 168, 192, 196, 197, 199, 200
eighteenth century, 8
Electoral College, 1, 12, 24, 65
elitism, 2, 9, 11, 21, 161
oppression; *also see* racism; sexism, 2
group oppression; *also see* racism; sexism, 3
equality, 9, 23, 24, 40, 41, 46, 47, 48, 50, 73, 97, 111, 161
equality, misinterpretation of, 47, 98, 160
ethnicity, 10, 18, 99, 130, 145, 146, 147, 193
Europe, 6, 8, 14, 30, 34, 35, 42, 152, 153, 155, 157, 159, 161, 175

F

family, 154
Faubus, Orval, 129
Fifth Amendment, 34
First Amendment, 7, 140, 163, 164
Florida, 65, 78, 79, 81, 82, 83, 84, 85, 92, 109, 170, 185
Florida Supreme Court, 79
Fredrickson, George M., 90, 137
freedom of speech, 2, 6, 8, 9, 101, 140
Freire, Paulo, 44
Freud, Sigmund, 3, 14

G

Galileo, 7
gay people, 2, 15, 16, 62
gender, 13, 23, 24, 50, 53, 60, 64, 84, 88, 134, 135, 196
genes, 39, 155
Georgia, 87, 88, 109, 186, 187
golden rule, 9, 46

government, 4, 5, 7, 9, 13, 28, 31, 67, 70, 98, 114, 123, 159, 161, 185

H

Hannah-Jones, Nikole, 21, 166, 167, 172, 180
Hawn, Matthew, 94
hierarchical society, 3, 7, 8, 16, 17, 36, 37, 50, 57
Hiroshima, 113
history, 2, 4, 5, 6, 10, 11, 18, 19, 20, 21, 22, 34, 35, 38, 40, 43, 50, 51, 54, 56, 68, 69, 71, 76, 84, 85, 87, 95, 96, 99, 110, 117, 119, 124, 141, 145, 152, 156, 158, 159, 169, 178, 179, 186, 190, 191, 192, 193, 197, 199, 201, 204, 205
Hitler, Adolf, 153

I

Idaho, 63
identity,, 41, 64, 84, 86, 134, 135, 156
indigenous peoples, 7, 12, 17, 36, 38, 118, 138, 139, 144, 149, 157, 159, 169, 174, 202, 203, 204
Iowa, 13, 124, 125, 130, 131, 133, 197, 198
Irving, Debby, 108

J

Jackson, John H., 114
Jackson, Luther P., 10, 170
James, Mary, 26
Jews, 7, 42, 152, 153
Jim Crow, 8, 11, 12, 13, 15, 21, 27- 33, 35, 41, 42, 50, 55, 63, 79, 88, 91, 96, 103, 109, 115, 119, 129, 144, 167, 177, 182
Jim Crow of the mind, 11, 12, 13, 15, 21, 63, 79, 88, 91, 96, 103, 115, 129
Johnson, Grace Hays, 10
Jones, Jacqueline, 143, 168

K

Kansas, 28, 30, 157, 158, 159, 177
Kansas City, Kansas, 28, 30, 157, 158, 159
Kentucky, 114, 115, 116, 157, 158, 159, 194, 195
Kluger, Richard, 44, 117, 123
Knudsen, Austin, Montana Attorney General, 45, 47, 55, 56, 139, 140, 141, 179, 180, 201
Ku Klux Klan, 95, 190

L

laborers, 20, 159
language, 11, 16, 39, 52, 54, 57, 155
legality, 45
Linnaeus, Carl, 36
Loving v. *Virginia*, 31, 174, 179
Lueger, Karl, 152, 153
lynching, 29, 32, 63, 168, 170

M

Maryland, 36, 174, 177
Massachusetts, 7, 36, 66
medicine, 32, 168
meritocracy, 57, 58, 75, 82, 98, 106, 110, 121, 127, 141, 147
Mexico, 67, 68, 183, 185
Mill, Harriot Taylor, 7, 164
Mill, John Stuart, 6
Mississippi, 63, 109
Montagu, Ashley, 39, 128, 168, 174
Montana, 13, 45, 55, 138, 139, 149, 201
Montgomery. Alabama, 109
monuments to slavery, 31, 69, 88, 95, 181, 184, 186, 187, 189
Murphy, Dervla, 148
myths, 6, 11, 14, 15, 40, 42, 43, 128

N

Netherlands, 7
New Hampshire, 13, 133, 134, 135, 136, 171, 199, 200
nineteenth century, 29, 30, 118, 152, 153
Noem, Kristi, South Dakota Governor, 145
North Dakota, 13, 149, 150, 182, 203, 204

O

Obama, Barack, 16, 168, 173
objectivity, 53, 54, 55, 56, 57, 58, 72, 82, 83, 99, 106, 141
Oklahoma, 118, 119, 120, 175, 177, 182, 195, 196
oppression; *also see* racism; sexism, 3, 5, 7, 9, 12, 13, 15 - 17, 22, 23, 25, 27, 29, 30, 36, 44, 53, 56, 76, 81, 99, 139, 155

P

patriotism, 58, 69, 70, 71, 76
Pilgrims, 7
Plato, 3, 14
Plessy v. *Ferguson*, 8, 28, 46, 164, 175, 179
Popper, Karl R., 49
poverty, 16, 87, 161
Princeton University, 30
privilege, 51, 94, 98, 125, 139
prohibitive concepts, 63
Providence (Rhode Island), 8
psychological distress, 75, 97, 106, 120, 126, 141, 146
public schools, 1, 4, 12, 15, 19, 20, 45, 48, 50, 57, 60, 61, 70, 76, 80 - 83, 85, 88, 96, 100, 115, 122, 127, 133, 134, 136, 150, 158
punishment, 61

R

race (in quotes), 10, 13, 14, 16 - 19, 22 - 28, 31 - 42, 45, 55, 59, 62, 64, 74, 75, 79, 80 - 84, 88, 89, 92, 94, 97 - 99, 105, 106, 110 - 112, 119,

120, 121, 125 - 128, 130, 134 - 136, 139 - 141, 145 - 147, 150, 153, 156, 157, 159, 165, 168, 179, 180, 182, 189, 192, 193, 195 - 199, 201, 204
racism, 2 - 6, 8, 9, 11, 14 - 19, 23, 25, 27, 29, 31, 32, 34, 35, 37, 39, 40 - 43, 45 - 47, 50 - 55, 57, 59, 60, 62, 65, 68, 70 - 76, 80 - 84, 86, 88, 89, 95 - 99, 104 - 108, 110 - 112, 115, 119, 120, 121, 124 - 127, 131 - 134, 136 - 141, 144 - 147, 149, 150, 152, 153, 156, 158, 162, 163, 164, 166, 168, 169, 171 - 173, 179, 191, 192, 197, 198, 199, 200, 203
rationality, 3, 6, 11, 14
religion, 7, 9, 15, 64, 98, 99, 130, 134, 135, 145, 146, 147
rhetorical tricks, 59, 79
Roe v. Wade, 5, 152
Roger Williams, 7, 162, 169
Roosevelt, Theodore, 29, 102, 168
Rosenberg, Alfred, 153
rubber band words, 58, 73, 74, 79, 80, 89
Rushdie, Salman, 151

S

Savannah, Georgia, 87
science, 6, 16, 17, 32, 39, 40, 42, 43, 53, 156

segregation, 2, 8, 12, 13, 20, 27 - 31, 45, 50, 115, 155, 157, 158
Seminoles, 78
seventeenth century, 7, 36
sexism, 2, 3, 5, 6, 9, 11, 14 - 16, 42, 43, 45, 46, 50 - 54, 57, 60, 62, 65, 70, 73, 74, 75, 76, 80, 81, 83, 88, 89, 97, 99, 104 - 107, 112, 119, 120, 124 - 127, 133, 134, 141, 145 - 147, 152, 164, 166, 173
social status; *also see* racism, 81
social status; *also see* racism, 125
social status; *also see* racism, 139
Shetterly, Margot Lee, 21
slavery; *also see* slaves, 2 - 5, 8, 11, 12, 16 - 18, 21, 23, 27, 28, 29, 32, 33, 35, 36, 38, 40, 41, 45, 51, 54 - 56, 67, 68, 69, 71, 73, 76, 78, 79, 87, 88, 91, 95, 103, 109, 111, 114 - 118, 124, 129, 133, 138, 144, 145, 149, 155 - 158, 169, 170, 171, 175, 177, 178, 179, 186, 188, 191, 195, 196, 200, 202, 203
slaves; *also see* slavery, 8, 16, 20, 23, 26, 29, 33, 34, 36, 37, 40, 44, 54, 56, 67, 68, 78, 87, 91, 103, 114, 118, 155, 157, 159, 169, 170, 183, 185, 186, 188
Somerset v. *Stewart*, 33, 176

South Carolina, 103, 104, 107, 109, 190, 191, 192
South Dakota, 13, 144, 145, 149, 174, 176, 202, 203
Spinoza, Baruch, 7, 165
state laws, 3, 4, 5, 8, 9, 11, 12, 15, 20, 21, 22, 24, 42, 43, 45, 46, 52, 53, 57, 60, 61, 79, 88, 114, 130, 133, 150, 152, 153, 158, 161, 180, 181
Supreme Court, 12, 28, 30, 31, 34, 47, 95, 152, 158
systematic racism, 125, 133, 149
systematic sexism, 125

T

teachers, 1, 12, 19, 30, 50, 51, 53, 54, 57, 59, 60, 61, 63, 70 - 76, 79, 80 - 83, 85, 89, 93, 94, 96, 99, 100, 104, 106, 107, 110, 112, 119, 120 - 122, 126, 130, 136, 141, 145, 146, 154, 157, 158, 200
Tennessee, 94 - 96, 100, 174, 189, 190
Texas, 65 - 77, 92, 183, 184, 185
The 1619 Project, 21, 54, 55, 62, 71, 83, 84, 116, 166, 172, 179, 180
Thirteenth Amendment, 8, 12, 33, 35, 68, 95, 114, 129, 138, 144, 149
Thurlow, Setsuko, 113

Trump, Donald, 16, 86, 168, 173
Tulsa, Oklahoma, 119, 196, 197
twentieth century, 8, 27, 28, 29, 37, 157

U

unconscious bias, 15, 27, 32, 50, 51, 52, 53, 74, 80, 88, 105, 112, 120, 126, 134, 140, 146
United States, 1 - 5, 7, 8, 11, 12, 15, 19, 20, 21, 23, 27, 28, 30, 32, 34, 38, 39, 42, 44, 45, 50, 51, 55, 61, 67, 70, 71, 73, 76, 78, 81, 84, 89, 91, 95, 98, 103, 108, 110, 111, 117, 119, 123, 125, 131, 137, 151 - 153, 155, 158, 159, 161, 164, 166, 168, 172, 173, 175, 176, 177, 180, 182, 183
United States House of Representatives, 1, 65
United States Senate, 1
United States Supreme Court, 8, 28, 31, 45, 46, 114, 158
University of Indiana, 30, 157
University of Kansas, 158
Utah, 63, 64

V

vagueness, 51, 60, 61, 62, 76, 112
values, 3, 8, 9, 11, 17, 22, 23, 24, 36, 64, 73, 98, 139
Vassar College, 30, 168

victims, 12, 16, 29, 30, 41, 47, 56
vigilantism, cultural, 60, 61, 62, 66, 75, 76, 84, 93, 100, 107, 121, 135
Virginia, 31, 36, 46, 54, 91, 92, 175, 187, 188, 189
Voting Rights Act of 1965, 31
voting, restriction of, 2, 13, 46, 69, 138, 160

W

Washington, Booker T., 20
Western culture, 14
white male supremacy, 3, 12, 13, 15, 18, 21 - 24, 50, 53, 62, 69, 124, 152

white supremacy, 18, 22, 23, 27, 28, 35, 40, 95
Williams, Roger, 7, 162, 169

women, 2, 5, 13, 14, 15, 16, 19 - 25, 36, 39, 40, 46, 47, 52, 56, 57, 62, 69, 112, 157, 160
women mathematicians, 21
women's right to their bodies, 5, 13, 15, 24, 30, 46, 52, 75, 77, 160, 161, 167, 182, 183
Woodrow Wilson, 30, 168
Woodward, C. Vann, 28

Y

Youngkin, Glenn, Virginia Governor, 92, 188, 189

THE AUTHOR

John L. Hodge's writings consist of books, book chapters, letters and a blog that pave the way towards a more humane society. He is the principal co-author of *Cultural Bases of Racism and Group Oppression: An Examination of Traditional "Western" Concepts, Values and Institutional Structures Which Support Racism, Sexism and Elitism* (1975). He is the author of "Democracy and Free Speech: A Normative Theory of Society and Government," Chapter 5 of *The First Amendment Reconsidered* (1982); "Equality: Beyond Dualism and Oppression," Chapter 6 of *Anatomy of Racism* (1990); *How We Are Our Enemy – And How to Stop: Our Unfinished Task of Fulfilling the Values of Democracy* (2011); *Dialogues on God: Three Views* (2012), *Overcoming the Lie of "Race": A Personal, Philosophical, and Political Perspective* (2017 – 2nd ed.), and *Presidential Racism: The Words of U.S. Presidents Since the Civil War and an Essay: The Enduring Anti-Democratic Disease Afflicting Us – And Its Cure* (2020).

He has an A.B. in mathematics from the University of Kansas (where he was awarded membership into Phi Beta Kappa), a Ph.D. in philosophy from Yale University, and a law degree (J.D.) from the University of California, Berkeley (Berkeley Law). In his long career beginning in the mid-1960s he was a draft counselor and peace intern with the American Friends Service Committee in Houston and Seattle; a college teacher and university professor mostly at California State University, East Bay; a Law Clerk for the Massachusetts Appeals Court; a Staff Attorney for the U. S. Court of Appeals for the First Circuit; and a lawyer for Massachusetts state agencies that provided health care, including Medicaid. He participated in the development of the Massachusetts model that was used nationally to create the Affordable Care Act (known as "Obamacare"). He lives with his wife, fiber artist Diane Franklin, in the Boston area.

For more information, go to JohnLHodge.com.

www.ingramcontent.com/pod-product-compliance
Lightning Source LLC
LaVergne TN
LVHW091251080426
835510LV00007B/211